THE CUP OF FURY

UPTON SINCLAIR
THE CUP OF FURY

CHANNEL PRESS INC., GREAT NECK, NEW YORK

I wish to thank the publishers of the following copyrighted works for permission to quote therefrom:

Jack London, *John Barleycorn* (Appleton-Century Crofts, Inc., 35 West 32nd Street, New York 1, N.Y.)

Susan Glaspell, *The Road to the Temple* (Ernest Benn, Ltd., 154 Fleet Street, London E. C. 4, England)

Van Wyck Brooks, *The Confident Years* (E. P. Dutton & Company, Inc., 300 Fourth Avenue, New York 10, N.Y.)

William Seabrook, *Asylum*; Louis Untermeyer, *Modern American Poetry* (Harcourt, Brace & Company, 383 Madison Avenue, New York 17, N.Y.)

Edna St. Vincent Millay, *A Few Figs From Thistles* (Harper & Brothers, 49 East 33rd Street, New York 16, N.Y.)

Brom Weber, Editor, *The Letters of Hart Crane, 1916-1932* (Hermitage House, Inc., 8 West 13th Street, New York 11, N.Y.)

Henry Mencken, *A Mencken Chrestomathy*; Robert H. Elias, *Theodore Dreiser, Apostle of Nature*; Charles Angoff, Editor, *The World of George Jean Nathan* (Alfred A.

Knopf, Inc., 501 Madison Avenue, New York 22, N.Y.)
William Seabrook, *No Hiding Place* (Copyright 1942);
Stanley Walker, *City Editor* (J. B. Lippincott Company, 227
South 6th Street, Philadelphia 5, Pa.)
John Malcolm Brinnin, *Dylan Thomas in America* (Little,
Brown & Company, 34 Beacon Street, Boston 6, Mass.)
Hart Crane, *Collected Poems of Hart Crane, Including The
Bridge* (Published by Liveright Publishers, New York; copy-
right 1933 Liveright, Inc.)
Isadora Duncan, *My Life* (Published by Liveright Publishers,
New York; copyright R 1955 Liveright Publishing Corpora-
tion, 386 Fourth Avenue, New York 16, N.Y.)
Ben Hecht, *A Child of the Century* (Simon & Schuster, Inc.,
630 Fifth Avenue, New York 20, N.Y.)
Helen Dreiser, *My Life With Dreiser* (World Publishing
Company, 2231 West 110th Street, Cleveland 2, Ohio)
Robert Straus and Selden D. Bacon, *Drinking in College*
(Yale University Press, 143 Elm Street, New Haven 7,
Conn.)

*I also want to thank the publishers of the following
periodicals for permission to quote from the indicated articles:*

Atlantic Monthly, "The Incorruptible Sinclair Lewis," by
Perry Miller (April, 1951)
New York Times, obituary on Maxwell Bodenheim (Febru-
ary 8, 1954)
New Republic, "The Violence of Dylan Thomas," by Hans
Meyerhoff (July 11, 1955)
The Reporter, "A Luncheon With Dylan Thomas," by Mary
Ellin Barrett (April 27, 1954)
World, Maclean-Burgess news story (January, 1954)

THE CUP OF FURY

1

No WRITER IN our century has known greater acclaim than an idolizing public accorded Jack London at the peak of his popularity. Whenever he made a public appearance, vast crowds swarmed to hear him speak. He was one of a very few whose work drew an enormous following in the popular magazines, and was equally admired by serious literary critics, sociologists, and philosophers. He had legions of friends in every country, and an unmatched zest for living. An unparalleled story-teller, London was also a social philosopher of the first rank, spearheading many of the great social and industrial reforms which by mid-century have become the law of our land.

In 1913, the year before World War 1, Jack London published a little book entitled *John Barleycorn*. It was a gallant work in which he told the story of a life of wild drinking, beginning incredibly enough at the age of five, and continuing more than thirty years. In this slim volume he described what he called "the Long Sickness" and "the White Logic" — respectively, the pessimism and the skepticism produced by alcoholism — and when he came to the end, he summed up his conclusions with these words:

Mine is no tale of a reformed drunkard. I was never a drunkard, and I have not reformed. . . No. . . I shall take my drink on occasion. With all the books on my shelves, with all the thoughts of the thinkers shaded by my particular temperament, I have decided coolly and deliberately that I should continue to do what I have been trained to want to do. I will drink — but oh, more skillfully, more discreetly than ever before. Never again will I be a peripatetic conflagration.

Thus, proudly, Jack London concluded his story. He went on with his drinking, "more skillfully, more discreetly," for two or three years. And then at the age of forty he gave his last word on the subject of liquor by taking his own life.

He was one of my cherished friends, a fellow worker in the cause of social justice; and although only a year and a half older than myself, a hero to me personally. I have never ceased thinking about him; I have never ceased to regret that I did not know how to help him. And recently I have come to believe that perhaps I can at least assist others by writing a parallel study of the effects of alcohol on the many drinking writers I have known.

As London did, I shall often talk in terms of "John Barleycorn" instead of employing the technical phraseology of current discussions of alcoholism. I do this because I believe it is sometimes easier to fix one's focus on a symbol or on a personification rather than on impersonal statistics and phrases.

I will write as one who has had but three or four sips of liquor in his life; as one who was early warned away from alcohol. It was my fate to be raised in a virtual sea of liquor. First it was my father. Then no fewer than three of my uncles — proud Southern gentlemen, one of them a naval hero. Then one friend after another, colleagues and writers, many of them famous and all of them destroying themselves.

I compile a list of the victims I have known, and there are seventy-five names; I should say that thirty of them are known to most literate Americans; a dozen are known throughout the literate world.

I say it is a frightful thing that so much of the talent and genius of America should have been distorted by alcoholic poisoning. These are indeed men and women who have to a great extent set the intellectual and moral tone of our time. They are among the few who have achieved fame and fortune; they have won both the critics and the readers. Most of them started with vision and courage, but in the end the example they give us is of sickness of mind and soul.

They have helped bring about an America in which people feel they "must" drink. And America is drinking, more than ever before in our recent history. In the old days we bought it in saloons; now we buy it in groceries, drugstores, package stores, drive-ins and state-operated establishments. A huge advertising subsidy brings the allurements of rye and bourbon, vodka and gin, rum and Scotch, bottled cocktails and "spiked" fruit-drinks before everybody in the land. At the same time we have a crime wave forever rising. Many of the criminals are youths, and some are children; their acts are frequently associated with drinking bouts.

Someone has to speak out on this subject. For recording

the sorrows and agonies of my fellow-writers I expect no applause, and am prepared to dodge the stale tomatoes. Let me say now, therefore, that it has never cost me the slightest effort to decline a drink; explicitly and thankfully, I claim no particle of credit or superiority because I escaped the clutches of liquor. Just as emphatically let me state that I do not point a finger to degrade memories and defame men; these were people who suffered from a dreadful disease. Their stories, I believe, may have the impact of an antitoxin.

I cannot help the old; I know, because I have tried again and again. They tell me they could quit if they wanted to, but they can't "want to." Even when they are in agony and want to escape, they need a drink first; and that first is never the last.

Now it is a question of giving information to the young. I tell myself that among the seventy-four percent of college students who drink today there may be a future Jack London or O. Henry, a future Sinclair Lewis or Scott Fitzgerald.

It is for them that I am writing. I will tell in this book what I have seen with my own eyes and heard with my own ears, often from the lips of the victims. First in Baltimore and then in Virginia, later in New York and then in many parts of California, it has been my fate to live among drinking people: novelists, poets, playwrights and stars of stage and screen. I have seen two-score of them go to their doom, eleven as suicides.

So much of what I write will be a story of sorrow, multiplying and increasing itself, that I want to begin it with a story of hope; I want to point to the promise of this book. And to do that, I must tell you a bit about myself.

I was brought up as an ardent little Episcopalian boy. At the age of fifteen I was teaching Sunday School classes at the Church of the Holy Communion in New York, and

I went to church every afternoon during Lent: not because I was told to, but because I wanted to. I read the Bible straight through, and its language and imagery became a part of me. I received from the church two gifts which I count priceless — personal habits of abstemiousness, and an attitude of moral earnestness toward the problems of human life.

When I set seriously to work to learn foreign languages, I chose the New Testament as my first textbook; not merely did it save me from frequent, interrupting dashes to a dictionary for help, but I found it fascinating to see how the golden words looked in Latin and Greek, French, German and Italian. I read it from Matthew to Revelation in each of these languages, and I commend the practice to students. As a result, many of the texts are as familiar to me as my own name, and you will find them scattered through most of my sixty-five books and numerous pamphlets.

I have never doubted that this is a spiritual universe; and if I cannot understand exactly how that can be, and how God works, it must be because God has chosen to have it that way. In my youth I experienced excitements which I took to be inspiration. I didn't know how or why they came, but it seemed as though a hand were lifting me up and guiding me. Even now, in my old age, I go out in my garden and walk, and a chapter of a new book I am writing unrolls itself in my mind. I cannot tell how it happens, but there it is: and it is always a marvelous thing to me. All problems of construction are answered, and all I have to do is remember the words until I have written them down. This much I can say, and be sure: that I am performing an act of creation, the very essence of life.

When I was running for Governor of California in 1934, some of my opponents found it politically useful to call me an "atheist." One old gentleman was prompted by these accusations to send me a long questionnaire, demanding that I fill it out. I was glad to oblige him. His first question was, "Do you believe in God?" My answer was, "Yes." He next demanded, "Define God." And I replied, "The infinite cannot be defined." I knew that this answer might not be satisfactory to my correspondent, but it seemed clear to me that since God is Spirit, and infinite, He has not dimensions which can be neatly defined in a questionnaire. I took it that God, who has put me on this earth and given me power to understand and seek for understanding, meant for me to use it.

I had what I believed was a God-given vision of a world without poverty and war, destroyers of God's children, and I was laboring to make that vision real to my fellow men. Often I failed, lamentably, in my efforts. There came poverty, debt, illness, sorrow. Sometimes I felt that I had made a fool of myself; sometimes I was tempted to imitate Job's impatient advisors, and blame God for the way He treated me. In this mood, it was no longer enough to say that I believed this to be a spiritual universe; I had to make the words real to myself, I had to make them count in my own troubled life. I had to reexamine what I believed about prayer. I had learned the ancient Dominican prayer that "to work is to pray," and I worked; but it was not enough. Now I asked God to give me courage, resolution, and hope—and behold, I had these things, these wonderful gifts of the mind and spirit without which men are as the "dumb, driven cattle."

And it was the same with my beloved wife. For two decades she stood at my side, doing the work of several persons: making me a home and keeping it; revising my manuscripts, and urging me not to write so hastily; keeping me out of debt, or trying to; warding off the parasites and cheats who swarm about every reformer and public man.

Then her health began to break under the strain, and she took me off to a hiding-place and set out in search of her own soul. She read the leading scientists of our time: Jeans and Eddington, Whitehead and Carrel, all of them religious men. She read everybody who could throw light on the mysteries of the human soul, from Gerald Heard to Mrs. Eddy. She met William McDougall and J. B. Rhine and Albert Einstein, and discussed these questions with them, knowing that each of these men possessed a deep belief in God.

She learned a better way of prayer, and she learned to control her own mind in many useful ways: she won back her health, and would have kept it, except that again and again she tried to do more than any one woman could do.

A year or more ago she had a heart attack, the kind which doctors call "congestive." She was in terrible pain, and I thought she was dying; she thought it too, and she could not bear to think of what fate she would leave me to, alone.

In that crisis I did not stop to argue any theological questions. I did not debate the exact nature and definition of God with the theologians.

I prayed. I prayed just one thing, over and over and over. I prayed, "Dear God, help her! Dear God, save her!"

I prayed alone and incessantly, all that dreadful night. We were in a remote place and there was no doctor; no one to help us, no one to know; just God. You perhaps know the story of the Frenchman who prayed, "Dear God, if there be a God, save my soul, if I have a soul." I did not follow his example. I did not put in any "if's."

My wife declares that these prayers saved her life. The skeptics will say, of course, that she heard my prayers, and that the realization of my love and need revived her will to live and increased her ability to endure the pain. I won't argue with the skeptics. I will simply say that God made psychology, too, just as He made all other things — the human mind as well as the human body. And the way they work is the way He works. If prayer gives you courage and hope and love, then what I say is "Thank God!"

There, in this book of sorrow, lies the hope.

I am able to say to alcoholics: Prayer will help you, your own prayer and others'.

This is what Alcoholics Anonymous has found, and what they tell themselves and all who come to them for help.

They invite the drinker and the drunkard "to believe that a Power greater than ourselves can restore us to sanity." They invite those in the depths of despair and dissolution "to make a decision to turn your will and your life over to God as you understand Him."

I put before the public this tragic record of a half-century of American genius, twisted and tortured by alcohol. I ask that it be read with one fact always in the back of the reader's mind: the fact that three out of four of the students in college today are drinkers. I want them to know this story; I want them to see that the chains of the despot are easy to assume when one is young, and of unimaginable hardness to break in later years.

I ask if this is what they want out of life.

And I offer them hope.

2

I BEGIN THIS personal part of my book by quoting the first three pages of a novel called *Love's Pilgrimage*, published almost fifty years ago. It has an old-fashioned ring to it, I'm afraid; yet there is probably no better way for me to show how my attitudes toward alcohol were formed. I wrote *Love's Pilgrimage* soon after my father's death. This story is one which we lived.

It was the Highway of Lost Men.

They shivered, and drew their shoulders together as they walked, for it was night, and a cold, sleety rain was falling. The lights from saloons and pawnshops fell upon their faces— faces haggard and gaunt with misery, or bloated with disease. Some stared before them fixedly; some gazed about with furtive and hungry eyes

as they shuffled on. Here and there a policeman
stood in the shelter, swinging his club and watching them as they passed. Music called to them from
dives and dance-halls, and lighted signs and flar-
ing-colored pictures tempted them in the entrances
of cheap "museums" and theatres; they lingered
before these, glad of even a moment's shelter.
Overhead the elevated trains pounded by; and
from the windows one could see men crowded
about the stoves in the rooms of the lodging
houses, where the steam from their garments made
a blur in the air.

Down this highway walked a lad, about
fifteen years of age, pale of face. His overcoat
was buttoned tightly about his neck, and his
hands thrust into his pockets; he gazed around
him swiftly as he walked. He came to this place
every now and then, but he never grew used to
what he saw.

He eyed the men who passed him; and when
he came to a saloon he would push open the door
and gaze about. Sometimes he would enter, and
hurry through, to peer into the compartments
in the back; and then go out again, giving a wide
berth to the drinkers, and shrinking from their
glances. Once a girl appeared in a doorway, and
smiled and nodded to him. Her wanton black
eyes haunted him, hinting unimaginable things.

Then, on a corner, he stopped and spoke to
a policeman. "Hello!" said the man, and shook
his head — "No, not this time." So the boy
went on; there were several miles of this Highway, and each block of it the same.

At last, in a dingy bar-room, with saw-dust strewn upon the floor, and the odor of stale beer and tobacco-smoke in the air — here suddenly the boy sprang forward, with a cry: "Father!" And a man who sat with bowed head in a corner gave a start, and lifted a white face and stared at him. The man rose unsteadily to his feet, and staggered to the other; and fell upon his shoulder, sobbing.

The man clung to him, weeping and pouring out the flood of his shame. "I have fallen again. I am lost, my son, I am lost!"

The occupants of the place were watching the scene with dull curiosity; and the boy was trembling like a wild deer trapped. "You must come home."

"You still love me, son?"

"Yes, Father, I still love you. I want to try to help you. Come with me."

Then the boy would gaze about and ask, "Where is your hat?"

"Hat? I don't know. I have lost it." The boy would see the torn and mud-stained clothing, the poor old pitiful face, eyes bloodshot and swollen; and the skin that once had been rosy was now a ghastly, ashen gray. He would choke back his feelings, and grip his hands to keep himself together.

"Come, Father, take my hat, and let us go."

"No, my son. I don't need any hat. Nothing can hurt me — I am lost! Lost!"

So they would go out, arm in arm; and while they made their progress up the Highway, the man would pour out his remorse, and tell the story of his weeks of horror.

Then, after a mile or so, he would halt.

"My son!"

"What is it, Father?"

"I must have something to drink."

"No, Father!"

"But, my boy, I can't go on! I can't walk! You don't know what I'm suffering!"

"No, Father!"

"I've got the money left—I'm not asking you, I'll come right with you — on my word of honor I will!"

And so they would fight it out — all the way back to the lodging-house where they lived, and where the mother sat and wept. And here they would put him to bed, and lock up his clothing to keep him in; and here, with drugs and mineral-waters, and perhaps a doctor to help, they would struggle with him, and tend him until he was on his feet again. Then, with clothing newly-brushed and face newly-shaven, he would go back to the world of men; and the boy would go back to his dreams.

I cannot remember any time so far back that my father was not a drinking man. He was in fact a drinking man before my mother married him. Her family had opposed the match for that reason, but he made promises, and she accepted them.

He was handsome, gay, and charming; Virginia-born, he settled in Baltimore immediately after the Civil War. His grandfather was Commodore Sinclair, who commanded the

Congress, the first frigate built by the United States government. The Commodore was the founder of the Annapolis Naval Academy, and was one of the founders of the Democratic Party.

The Commodore's son was Commander Arthur Sinclair of the United States Navy, later of the Confederate Navy. This Arthur—my grandfather—commanded one of the vessels in the squadron of Commodore Perry when it opened Japan to the outside world in 1853. In his boyhood he had served as a midshipman alongside another lad, David Farragut. They came from Norfolk and remained the closest of friends until the Civil War broke out. They were captains then, and when the conflict began, they shut themselves up in Arthur's study and argued for a day and a night about the aims and principles of each side. Neither was able to convince the other: Farragut moved North and achieved fame at the Battle of Mobile Bay, while Arthur took command of a Confederate blockade-runner carrying cotton to England. Union warships were waiting for him outside the port of Liverpool on his last trip; he tried to make his way out on a stormy night, and the ship went ashore on the rocks. Arthur was drowned. He was one of a large family who served under the Confederate flag; indeed, I had eight uncles and cousins who fought for the South.

Those of the family who survived the war were left without property. My father retained his pride as a Southern gentleman, but little else. He became a salesman for a wholesale liquor concern. Since it would have been bad business to refuse to patronize his own wares, this was an unfortunate occupation for him to choose.

We were always poor. We lived in one room in a Baltimore lodging house, and I can remember sleeping across the foot of the bed in which my parents slept. Then Father would be off on what was called a "spree." Our finances would fall so low that we could not even pay the landlady, and would be forced to go and stay in the home of my maternal grandfather, who was secretary-treasurer of the Western Maryland Railroad. There was abundance here, and even some elegance; and if you have read any of my novels, you can see why they deal with the contrast between poverty and riches in America.

Grandfather Harden lived in a four-story brick house on Maryland Avenue, above what was then called "The Boundary." A one-horse streetcar rolled by the door, and every morning except Sunday he would board the same car and ride to his office. He would return in the early afternoon for a two o'clock dinner, riding downtown again after lunch to finish his day's duties. He had a silver service which he put into a wicker basket every night and carried up to his bedroom for safety. And he gave terrapin suppers: I still remember those large and lively turtles in the back gardens. A Negro approached them warily and drove a steel fork through their heads, then chopped the heads off. At these parties no liquor was served, for Grandfather was a deacon of the Methodist church, and in his library were bound volumes of the *Christian Herald*, full of moral pictures which provided me with entertainment even before I taught myself to read.

I can see him now in my mind's eye. Grandfather Harden was a large, stoutish gentleman whose red-colored hair grew from his chin instead of on the top of his head. He was the kindest man you can imagine, and most upright; but don't imagine that he could get away from John Barleycorn! No, for he had a son, and his own deep religious principles had failed to affect that son. Maybe it was an over-indulgent mother, or perhaps the temptations of Baltimore's fashionable society, or possibly the example of his classmates in school — I never knew, because my Uncle Harry was a "drinking man" before I was born, and he never spoke frankly with me about his life.

One of my earliest and most vivid memories: I could not have been more than three or four years old. I was sleeping in a front bedroom on the top floor, and in the middle of the night was awakened by loud voices. I got out of bed in the canton-flannel nightgown which I wore, and toddled to the head of the stairs. The stairs went down in a circle and the sounds came plainly up the stairwell. A violent argument was going on at the front door. Uncle Harry was drinking, and Grandfather was trying to keep him from going out to do more drinking. Grandfather must have been trying to hold him by force, but Uncle Harry broke away and left — and what grief he left in his father's soul you can imagine.

Uncle Harry would go off on his drinking sprees regularly, and would lose one position after another. Finally he got a job with a brother-in-law who had started a bonding business in New York (I shall be telling you about this Uncle Bland before long). There, too, Harry would be discharged, then forgiven, then taken back again on the basis of new promises; but these were vows and assurances which, of course, he could never keep. He had been an athlete, a magnificent specimen of a man, handsome, gay, with a hearty laugh. Then at the age of forty, Uncle Harry bought himself a pistol, sat on a bench in Central Park, and put a bullet through his head.

Nor was he the last. Next was my Uncle Arthur Sinclair (the Third), my father's oldest brother. At the age of twenty-four he had served as Fifth Lieutenant on the *Alabama*, a Confederate commerce raider, during the Civil

War. His two children, a boy and a girl, were among my playmates in the Baltimore days. Later in his life Arthur wrote a book, *Two Years on the Alabama*, which is a valued historical record. I never saw him under the influence of liquor, but I heard the sad story of the family from my mother, and I was told that he too died an inebriate in an institution.

Next, my "Uncle Pow." His name was Powhatan Montague, and he boasted of being a descendant of Pocahontas. He came from Richmond to Baltimore and married one of my father's sisters. He had a kind, long-suffering wife, and two daughters who were also among my playmates, first in Baltimore and then in New York. When we were four or five years old we were romping, Lelia and I, and I put a pillow on Lelia's head and sat on it, having no idea of doing any harm. When they pulled me off, her face was purple. Fortunately, though, this event did not keep Lelia from growing up to become a famous beauty. After her marriage, she befriended a half-orphaned niece, launched her in Washington society, and then saw her go to England and become the Duchess of Windsor. That is a story I shall tell later on.

Uncle Powhatan was another big, handsome fellow, with a black moustache and a hearty laugh. He was full of mischief. "Pow, you devil!" my mother would exclaim, and he would be delighted. Pow was made for conviviality. He liked to prepare things in a chafing-dish, and whenever it was possible he would put what he called a "stick" in them.

You can see how I walked through life with drinkers and drunkards at my side. My father lived until I was thirty, and all that time I had him in my thoughts and often on my hands. I did everything I could for him; I took him to church, I took him to clergymen, I made an effort to interest him in reading. I recall that I once brought him the novels of Walter Scott, and they got along beautifully together, having exactly the same notions of gentility.

Let me try to bring before your eyes more clearly and vividly this kind and most pitiable Southern gentleman. My father was about five-feet-six, I would judge, and well filled-out. He wore a little pointed brown moustache, and his complexion was rosy. He laughed easily and was of a sociable disposition; this, I fear, is what trapped him. He took great care of his person, and was what they called a "swell dresser." His feet were small, and he was proud of them, taking them to be a sign of aristocracy. He would gaze down at a pair of tight little shoes, and he had words to describe them — they were "nobby," they were "natty," they were "neat."

He gave a great deal of attention to fashion, and also to food. What was the size and flavor of Blue Point oysters as compared with Lynnhaven Bays? Why was it impossible to obtain properly-cooked food north of Baltimore? What was the wearing quality of patent-leather shoes as compared with calfskin? Was there any fusel-oil in aged-in-the-wood whiskey? Would the straw hats of next season have high or low brims? Where had the Vanderbilts obtained the fifty-thousand-dollar slab of stone which formed the pavement in front of their Fifth Avenue palace? Wherein lay the superiority of Robert E. Lee over all other generals of history? These were the questions which occupied the mind of my stout little father.

He was so considerate, so good, and so utterly pathetic. In all the years I argued and pleaded with him, I cannot recall that I ever heard an angry answer from him. But nothing could save him. He was a traveling salesman, a "drummer," and every deal began with one drink and ended with another and another. He would make all sorts of vows and resolutions; he would "drink only beer," he would "never drink until evening" — but always in the end he would disappear, and then I would have to go and find him. The time came when we could no longer handle him at home, and I had to take him to a Catholic hospital where the good nuns had strong men at call.

It seems to me that my father could have been so happy, and we so happy with him, if only there had been no alcohol in the picture. Yet it was as if there were a doom upon him; he could not resist it. I would discuss his problem with him, and tears would come into his eyes and mine; he would make promises, but he could not keep them. As I remember it, he never went "off" while he was on his travels. When he had to make train connections and register at hotels and have his samples brought to a room and displayed for the customers, he was simply too busy, too excited to drink.

No, it was when he returned to the city and had to meet customers, entertain them, and drink with them that he would go "off." Sometimes he would be gone for a week or two before we found him. And when he came out of the hospital his complexion would look like soft dough, and his hands would be shaking so that he could take only a half-cup of coffee at a time. And my mother would be occupied long hours in keeping him supplied with it. He would try to shave himself — it was in the days before the safety razor — and he would cut himself. It was one of the signs by which I learned to know an alcoholic: the fresh nicks on doughy cheeks and chin.

You understand that there was then no known cure for alcoholism, no proved method of treatment. All one could do with a victim was to keep him full of coffee, and hide his clothes so that he could not escape. If the police got him, they just locked him up and let him suffer it out. There was a thing called "the Keeley cure," but my father was afraid of it; he knew a man who had taken it and had suffered greatly. So things went from bad to worse, until I reached the age of thirty. I happened to be in New York, working, and there came a telephone call from a public hospital; my father had died there in delirium tremens.

Life is a mystery, strange beyond all telling. My inebriate father would have approved this book. When he was beginning to drink he would say, "It is my only consolation." But when he was getting over it, he would say liquor was a curse. I can hear him moaning: "If only I had never touched it!" I leave that as his epitaph.

3

WHEN I was eight years old we moved to New York. We lived in a place which was called a family hotel, but which was really a large boarding house that had been made by joining together four old brownstone residences on West 19th Street. It was kept by a Colonel Weisiger from Virginia, and was frequented entirely by Southern people. The occupants were colonels, majors and captains from the Civil War days, and their families, all of them more or less impoverished by that war. There was no bar and no public drinking. It was a decorous place, even as every place in their dearly-loved South had been decorous when ladies were present. But of course the gentlemen brought liquor to their rooms.

Nearly a half-century later I described the Weisiger boarding house in a novel, *The Wet Parade*. A Negro porter named Taylor Tibbs worked in it, and every afternoon one of his duties was to go to the corner saloon and bring back two pails of beer for Colonel Weisiger. One influence of the beer was evident to my eye, for the old gentleman weighed a bloated two hundred and fifty pounds. The Colonel and his wife were generous people, and when we were in financial distress they would patiently wait for their money.

In the Weisiger house I heard much talk about liquor, which was always in the thoughts of these Southern gentlemen when not in their stomachs. Nowadays the ladies are drinking too, but in those days they were suffering only from the effect it had on their households.

I remember one young man who was never more than two-thirds sober. He was what the English call a "remittance man" — his family in the South paid him to stay in New York. And never shall I forget old Major Waterman, who caused me one of the most embarrassing moments of my young life.

One evening I was placed at a table with the Major and two young ladies. The venerable warrior started telling of an incident which had taken place that day. "I was walking along the street and I met Jones. 'Come in and have a drink,' said he, and I of course replied, 'No, thank you' —"

What was to be the end of that story I shall never know. "Oh, Major Waterman!" I burst out, obviously convinced that the Major would never and indeed could never say "No" to a drink. There followed an appalled silence. Terror gripped my soul as the old gentleman turned his bleary eyes upon me. "What do you mean, sir? Tell me what you mean!"

I was a brat, of course, and I deserved the lesson. The old gentleman's cheeks were inflamed and his nose had purple veins in it, but I could scarcely mention these as proof of his never-ending imbibing. All I could do was sit silent like a hypnotized rabbit as he bellowed, "I wish to have an answer, sir! What do you mean by that remark?"

I still have, as one of my weaknesses, the tendency to speak first and think afterwards; but the memory of Major Waterman has helped me on the way to reform. And I have since learned that alcoholism is a disease, that its victims need help, not ridicule.

In New York there was a saloon on every other corner. The one on Sixth Avenue, near the Weisiger household, was called "Sandkuhl's." The proprietor must have been a kind man, for he loaned money to certain gentleman customers. Some twenty years after my father's death, I received a letter from a Baltimore life insurance company, telling me that my father had owned a policy for two hundred dollars, and had assigned it to a man named Sandkuhl. Could I help them, they asked, in finding this man?

Thus even from the grave, my father continued his payments to the liquor manufacturers and their army of distributors!

I lived in New York for two years before I was permitted to attend school. I had taught myself to read at the age of five, using alphabet blocks, and a doctor warned my mother that this was "precocious," that I should be made to "rest my mind." And so I was ten years old before I went to a classroom for the first time. But after this delayed beginning, I went through the whole primary and grammar school process in two years. Still too young to go on to college, I was forced to repeat the last year of high school— the major purpose, I assume, being to keep me out of mischief.

It was at college that my life assumed direction and aim; at college that I decided to "become a writer." And since this book will essentially be the story of other writers with whom I have worked and lived, wonderful men and women whose sadly-beclouded lives were linked at one time or another with mine, I shall on occasion pause to tell you about myself: how I came to know them, strive with them, and live closely with them. I think you will be amused when you see how the little acorn of envy and emulation which led me into the literary life has since grown into an oak, with so many branches (I sometimes think!) that it threatens to become top-heavy.

The College of the City of New York was situated in an old brick building on East Twenty-third Street; I entered it a week before I was fourteen.

In my class in college was a Jewish boy by the name of Simon Stern, whom I had come to know well because we lived in the same neighborhood, and often walked home together. Simon wrote a short story; and one day he entered the class in triumph, announcing that his story had been accepted by a monthly magazine published by a Hebrew orphan home.

Straightway I was stirred to emulation. If Simon could write a story, why could not I? And so I wrote a story about a pet bird. For years it had been my custom every summer to take young birds from the nest and raise them. They would know me as their only parent, and were charming pets. Now I put one of these birds into an adventure, making it serve to prove the innocence of a colored boy accused of arson. I mailed the story to *Argosy*, one of the two Munsey publications issued in those early days, and the story was accepted. Price — $25.00! You can imagine that I was an insufferable youngster on the day the letter arrived; especially so to my friend Simon Stern, who had not been paid for his story.

Simon and I went into partnership and wrote an adventure novel — about which I cannot remember one thing, not even the title. Together we visited the offices of Street and Smith, publishers of "thrillers" for boys, and met one of the editors, who was amused to have two fifteen-year-old boys in short pants announce themselves as "joint authors of a novel." He read it, and did not accept it; but he did hold out hope to us, and suggested that we write another thriller, one better suited to his needs. We agreed to do so; and to the consternation of the editor, came back in a week with the new novel complete.

I am not sure what became of that story. The partnership dissolved, however, and during the ensuing summer I set to work on my own on a full-length novel of adventure. I am embarrassed now to realize how striking a resemblance it bore to *Treasure Island* — the key difference being that my book took place on land. It had to do with an effort by some returning "forty-niners" to find hidden gold before they were killed by Indians. *The Prairie Pirates* was the title, and I don't know if the manuscript survives; but I recall reading it at some later date, and being impressed by my idea of "sex-appeal" at the age of sixteen or seventeen. The hero had accompanied the beautiful heroine all the way from California, and rescued her many times from Indian marauders and treacherous half-breeds; finally he told her blushingly that he loved her. And then, having obtained permission, "he placed upon her forehead a holy kiss."

At about this time my father's condition had become so bad that I found it necessary to earn money; and one way in which I succeeded was by writing jokes. I read the joke pages in the newspapers daily, just as I read everything I could get hold of, and someone told me they paid a dollar apiece for such jokes. I tried, and found this to be true.

Joke-writing interested me. I had listened to my elders telling jokes, and had laughed whether I understood them or not. Now joke-writing took hold of me like an obsession. I thought up jokes as I walked on the street, while I ate my meals, after I went to bed at night, and when I opened my eyes in the morning. When I passed an Irishman I thought about Irish jokes; and the same with soldiers and tramps. When I went to the country with my mother, I wrote jokes about farmers. When I met a missionary I wrote jokes about missionaries and cannibals. I didn't write Jewish jokes, but only because Simon Stern monopolized that market!

I also wrote for my college magazine, without financial profit, but for the sheer fun of it. I have before me the bulky scrapbook into which my mother pasted these contributions, and all the jokes I sold. The magazine was called the *Phrenocosmian*, which means that it belonged to the Mind Cosmos, and that may account for the piece of erudition which I am about to put before you.

MY BELOVED VALENTINE

Desiring to promulgate my erotic cogitations,
   When Luna's coruscations lit the polyphloes-
      boean sea,
I sought my classic cubicle for nascent lucubra-
   tions
      To asseverate encomiastic sentiments for
         thee.
But in my contumacious Pegasus of assinine fa-
   tuity
      My diatribe, so truculent, oscitancy did
         cause,
And my calcarate titillations, cataclysms salta-
   tory;

> Disappeared my youthful fervor in the disceptation's pause.
> So from multifarious synonyms, with onerous defloration
> My penchant I manifested for the sesquipedalian line.
> Circumstances circumambient deserve consideration,
> So animadvert gently on my verdant valentine.

I kept a record, and my joke-writing brought in four dollars and a half a week. Three went for food at a boarding house, a dollar and a quarter for a fourth-story, back-hall bedroom — and that left me twenty-five cents for laundry. I never bought anything else, not even a newspaper for a penny.

So you can believe that I had neither time nor money for what is called "college life." I recall that a tall and impressive classmate approached me on the subject of joining a fraternity. I didn't know what one was, and when I learned that it cost money, I didn't have any.

Nearly all the students I met came from poor families, many of them foreigners and most of them Jewish. They were bent on improving their position in the world, and they worked hard. Years later, when my own son wanted to go to college, I let him earn his own way.

Thus, my contacts with whiskey-drinkers during this period were only through my father and my poor Uncle Harry, who at this time lived in the same Harlem lodging house as my mother and I. I had by now moved off into worlds of which this uncle knew nothing, and he advised me to "quit scribbling and get a job." But he did not follow my advice about his drinking, nor did I follow his about writing.

About the time of my graduation from the City College, at the age of eighteen, I received a letter from the Street and Smith editor, asking me to visit his office. The firm was planning a new "half-dime library," called the *Army and Navy Weekly*, each issue containing two stories — one of West Point life and the other of Annapolis life. They would be read by messenger boys, newsboys — all boys, in fact, who could be lured to part with five cents by a thrilling color picture on the cover. The editor himself was going to "do" Annapolis, and would I care to make a try for the West Point job? This of course, was like hearing a brass band coming down the street; and I wasn't merely going to follow it, like all the other boys — I was going to be the drum-major!

I accepted without hesitation. I had grown tired of joke-writing, and here was something with more body to it, and also more money — an increasingly important factor, since my father was becoming less and less dependable as a provider for the family.

Each of the new stories was to contain about eight thousand words, and would be paid for at the sumptuous and secure rate of one-third of a cent per word. Twenty-five dollars a week!

I consulted a clergyman friend, Mr. Moir, and it happened that he knew an officer of the Military Academy; and shortly I had a fine letter of introduction. I took a West Shore train the next day, watched the sights of the Hudson River, got off at the little town of Garrison, put up at a small and cheap hotel, and then walked to the Academy. I was kindly received by Mr. Moir's friend, who introduced me to several of the cadets.

They were marvels of grey-uniformed spickness and spanness; and I think they found something intriguing about a writer so very young, so small and seedy in contrast. I remember one magnificent specimen of military manhood, to whom I remarked that I would need a hero for my stories; replied he, with the utmost gravity, "I could serve for your hero. I am the head of the senior class, I am at the top in scholarship, and I am captain of the football team." I told him that I would be happy to use him as my model; unfortunately I don't remember his name, and sometimes wonder what became of him in World War I, and whether by chance he was one of the high commanders of World War II.

In any event, I wandered over the length and breadth of the Academy, fixing the local color in my mind. I admired the spacious grounds, set on a wide bluff where the great river narrows and makes a curve. I studied the impressive buildings which were scattered about, and learned their names and style of architecture. I stood by the great parade ground and watched the grey-clad figures of my country's young fighting men in training for war, executing complicated maneuvers, their legs moving with precision like the levers in a long weaving machine. I admired the bright foliage of the woods, walked on "Lovers' Lane," studied the ancient and honorable artillery, and gazed at the long view up the blue river. I collected the literature of the famous institution, learned the conditions of admission for candidates, and all the other rules and regulations. I asked a thousand questions, went back to the hotel at night, and filled a notebook with details. Then I returned to my hall bedroom in New York, and started scribbling with a pencil on cheap copy paper. With a flourish I wrote:

MARK MALLORY'S HEROISM:
Or, First Steps Toward West Point
by
Lt. Frederick Garrison, U.S.A.

This was the pen-name which had been assigned to me, and I never stopped to wonder whether or not there might be such a real person. I began: "CHAPTER ONE, *Two Candidates*." And the opening words were: "Is this seat engaged?"

The first scene took place in a railroad train in a depot at Omaha. Seated together were two young men; and as the train chugged out of the depot, they fell to chatting. Both, it turned out, were on their way to seek admission to West Point. One already had his appointment to the Academy; the other — Mark Mallory — soon realized with shock and dismay that his new friend had received his appointment *from Mark's own district*! And this meant that Mark would have to wait several years for another chance to enter the Point. (But wait, dear reader; don't despair. Fate was kind to our hero.)

Chapter Two was titled *What Happened to the Pacific Express*. And what happened was a terrible train wreck, in which Mark's new friend was so badly hurt that he could not continue his trip to West Point. Mark, however, escaped; and so was present when an old farmer rode up to the scene of the wreck. The farmer and the Governor of the State — who was on the train — began this conversation:

"Can't you get help?" demanded the Governor.

"Ain't nobody here t'help."

"Where's the nearest town?"

"Grangers, thirty miles from here."

"Good Lord!"

"There's a telegraph station ten miles from here —" the old man added.

"Ah!"

"But the operator ain't there. He goes over at night to Grangers."

"That settles it!" cried the Governor. "That settles it! Oh, if only we had a telegraph operator! He could save a dozen lives. But it's —"

"*Give me the horse!*"

The Governor stopped abruptly and faced about. The speaker was a tall young man coming over from the train. His face was pale now; but there was resolution in his eyes.

"You want a telegraph operator," he said. "Give me the horse."

That, of course, was Mark Mallory; and he not only rode the wild and dangerous horse called "Tiger," but he got to the station and sent a message which brought help to the injured. Then he rushed a full and exclusive account of the accident involving the Governor's train to the New York *Globe* and received a check for five hundred dollars in payment. Thus he could not only win the appointment to the U.S. Military Academy, but could also provide for his aged and impoverished mother.

The Mark Mallory stories were successful indeed from the point of view of the publishers. The editor told me that the great Mr. Smith of Street and Smith had asked him, "Has that young fellow been through West Point?" and the reply was, "Yes, he went through it in three days."

The stories were successful from my point of view, too,

because they made me a living, and enabled me to take care of my own impoverished (but not aged) mother. They are successful from the point of view of the book collector, because they sold for five cents a copy fifty-eight years ago, and now bring five dollars a copy. The only harm they may have done is set forth by my friend Van Wyck Brooks in his excellent book, *The Confident Years.* He writes:

"Upton Sinclair . . . supported himself by turning out pulp-novels, the 'half-dime' romances that Dreiser was employed to edit a few years later, and this perhaps gave him the fatal facility and established the commonplace style that he scarcely ever transcended as a serious writer."

As time went on, the battleship *Maine* was sunk in the harbor of Havana, and our country went to war with Spain. My West Point hero was graduated from the Military Academy at once; and there was I, in my hall bedroom in New York, outwitting spies and engaging vicariously in all kinds of hair-raising experiences. When people asked me what my job was I would answer, "Killing Spaniards." I thought nothing of sinking a whole fleet of enemy torpedo boats to achieve a climax.

Before long my editor found himself too busy to continue his own stint; he invited me to take over the Annapolis job also. I made the trip to Maryland, "went through Annapolis in three days," and came back and wrote twice as hard. After a year or more, I took on still another task for the firm; I wrote a monthly paper-book called the *Columbia Library.* By then I was turning out eight thousand words a day. Professional hacks may find this hard to believe, but it is so. I no longer wrote by hand; I employed two stenographers and kept them busy on alternate days, or rather nights, from seven o'clock until nine or ten. By the time I finished these three or four years of servitude, I had produced a volume of material equal in bulk to the writings of Sir Walter Scott.

Now I set out to write a serious novel; there was a lot of talk in those days about the "Great American Novel," and I undertook to provide it. When the publishers were unappreciative, I borrowed two hundred dollars from my Uncle Bland and published the book myself.

It didn't sell. But it made the first friendships I describe in this book; and thus I begin the stories of Jack London and George Sterling, O. Henry and Stephen Crane. I begin the story, essentially, of a group of brilliant and brave Americans who lived to write and died for wine.

4

A VOLUME OF short stories about the Klondike, written by a young writer named Jack London, had just been published. I read it and wrote to the author, sending him a copy of my own just-published book; thus there began a friendship by mail. We were two young social dreamers, eager to remake the world. We both read the *Appeal to Reason*, a weekly paper of political protest published in Girard, Kansas, by the redoubtable "one-hoss editor," J. A. Wayland. We were both certain that the Co-operative Commonwealth, a world without poverty, was coming soon. Thereafter when one of us wrote a new book, his first thought was to send it to the other; and always the other liked what he read.

And then there came a book from Jack with an inscription beginning, "I have a friend, the dearest in this world." The book was *The Testimony of the Suns* by George Sterling. I read it and found it magnificent poetry on the highest of themes. George loved Aldebaran and Betelgeuse as Milton loved Ormuz and Ind, the Stygian cave forlorn and the dark Cimmerian desert. Of course I wrote to George immediately, and another friendship began. I did not know that he too was a drinking man, and seven or eight years passed before I found it out. Some of the critics may have known it sooner, however; when he published *The Wine of Wizardry*, one said that it ought to have been called "The Wizardry of Wine."

As you read this book of mine you will find one after another of the great poets and novelists of America described, men and women whose talents should have been conserved for the benefit of all humanity. You will find them set down here as pitiful victims of alcohol; you will read my evidence that alcohol is perhaps our most persistent purveyor of agony and premature death. Critics of this approach to the problem of alcoholism may reply to me with the story of Abraham Lincoln and General Grant; people complained of Grant's drinking too much whiskey, and Lincoln replied: "Find out the name of the brand for me so that I can give it to my other generals!"

This makes a witty story, but you will be mistaken if you draw the conclusion that one can create genius with whiskey. I once asked George Sterling about this; he would know, I felt, if any man in the world could know. He answered, "If you write when you have been drinking, you think you have written the most wonderful thing in the world; but when you read it in the morning, you discover that it makes no sense." Great men are great not because of alcohol, but in spite of it.

My young colleagues were certainly great, and their work inspired me. I could no longer write "half-dime novels," because I had come to despise them; and when I did try, in order to eat, the editors told me that my tales were no longer any good. I picked up a few dollars here and there writing sketches, book reviews, and miscellaneous articles for magazines. I wrote a satirical novel called *Prince Hagen*. It was rejected by seventeen magazines and twenty-two publishing houses (which in itself took a year or two), but at last I found a publisher in Boston. The book earned two hundred dollars—less than the copying costs and the postage and express charges.

Out of this misery I wrote the diary of a young poet who was driven to suicide by despair. It was called *The Journal of Arthur Stirling,* and it made something of a sensation. Unfortunately in my ignorance I had signed a contract by which I would receive no royalties whatsoever until the book earned the cost of publication. I never got a dollar from it, and again was out the cost of having the manuscript typed. But I was learning to know the literary world.

I met the editors of the more intellectual magazines of that time—*Independent, Literary Digest, McClures.* They took an interest in me, gave me advice, and now and then—since I was pale and hungry-looking—invited me to lunch. The more worldly ones invited me to join them in a drink, and when I declined they were perhaps a little put out. They offered me cigarettes, and I did not smoke. I watched them quench their cigarettes in their coffee cups and take out their pencils and do what is called "doodling" on the white table-cloth. Their advice was that I should read their magazines, see what kind of material they published, and learn to write it. They published society love stories, adventure stories, stories which were exciting but never shocking, and which above all contained no social criticism.

One of the writers I was advised to imitate was O. Henry. His stories were gay, pathetic, human, and always had a trick ending, a snap-of-the-whip conclusion. I met an editor of *McClure's* who was helping to keep him alive. O. Henry had to be watched and guarded and *made* to write. He would promise a story by a certain date, and the editor would save the space for him; but the story did not come, and the editor would then be forced to send an assistant to watch over the writer, help him sober up, and make him sit down and work. He could not write anything bad, it seemed, but it was an agony for him to write at all.

Here was one more Southern gentleman in trouble with alcohol. His real name was William Sydney Porter, and I recall his tragic story with compassion. He was a bank clerk; one day some money was missing, and he was accused of embezzlement. Maybe he was guilty, or perhaps he was "taking the rap" for somebody else—he would never discuss the subject. He fled to Honduras; and Al Jennings, the famous train bandit who later reformed and wrote an autobiography, tells of meeting him there, half drunk and in jail. In the end, they both went home and served their sentences in the same prison. Many years later I put them both into a play, *Bill Porter,* which was produced in Hollywood.

O. Henry was dreadfully ashamed of this cloud of suspicion; also, he grieved for his wife, who had died of tuberculosis. He was proud, tormented, and frightened. Before long, death delivered him from his misery—at the age of forty-eight.

Another young writer I was advised to study was Stephen Crane, who had caused a tremendous sensation with a short novel titled *The Red Badge of Courage.* He followed it up with a novel about a girl of the streets, and he wrote eccentric poetry. And he too was a "drinking man."

Crane was obsessed by wars; I suppose that having imagined one with extraordinary vividness, he wanted to see if he had been right. He tried to get to Cuba in an old tub of a steamer which sank, and he barely escaped with his life; out of that came a story, *The Open Boat*. Later, when he reached Cuba, he horrified everybody by stepping out of the trenches and making himself a target for the shooting. He didn't care very much about living; he used to say that thirty-five years were enough for any man. He made only twenty-nine.

Crane fell ill in Cuba and took to drinking heavily as a "cure." He drank steadily. He was a very small man, only a hundred and twenty pounds. He was tubercular, and apparently the disease affected his intestines as well as his lungs. He was always hard up for money, and had a terrible time with editors and publishers. When he had a low character in one of his stories use the expression "b'Gawd" there was quite a controversy, and the expression came into print as "b'——." Crane was also interested in prostitutes, and he wrote a great deal about them in his books. The truth is the young novelist was a man of tender heart and of genuine social feeling; compared with another Crane whom we shall hear about in this book—Hart Crane—he appears as something of a saint.

It was impossible to live in the great metropolis and keep away from the sights and the smells and the miseries of alcohol. There were drinking places everywhere; there were dives for the poor, and elegant saloons in the hotels. There was the Knickerbocker at Broadway and Forty-second Street, and somebody invited me into the barroom; there I saw their famous painted lady hanging over the bar. I was introduced to a Western celebrity drinking at the Knickerbocker—a sheriff and friend of Teddy Roosevelt, Bat Masterson by name. He asked me what I would have, and I said lemonade; and of course that was queer. Nobody likes to be queer, and least of all a sensitive young writer who hasn't the price of a haircut.

What was talked about, though, was the same whether you were in the "Tenderloin" or the literary world. In those days everybody was reading *Mr. Dooley*, the story of a fictitious saloon-keeper on Archey Road in Chicago. A bit of a radical, Dooley made pungent remarks about how the Supreme Court followed the "illiction returns." *Mr. Dooley* was syndicated in the newspapers and afterwards published in book form; I remember how keenly my father and uncles read and appreciated him.

Finley Peter Dunne was the author, and I met him that day at the Knickerbocker. A rosy-faced genial Irishman whose conversation was as brilliant as his writing, he made a delightful companion. About that time Lincoln Steffens had published an interview with William Randolph Hearst, elaborately portraying the publisher as a man of mystery. I remember how Dunne chuckled as he explained Stef's mistake: Hearst, Dunne insisted, was scared stiff by the inquisition, and didn't know what to say. So he just looked at Stef and said nothing. This, apparently, made him "a man of mystery!"

Dunne became one of the founders and editors of the *American Magazine*; but alas, he would disappear for long periods, and there was no mystery about why he did this. Nor was it a mystery that his famous character was a saloon-keeper, for Dunne was a saloonkeeper's victim. He retired from the literary world long before his potential was half-realized.

In the movement of social reform, too, I came to know men of good heart who were enchained by the liquor habit. I remember attending a great mass meeting in New York, and there for the first time I met Eugene V. Debs. He had been a railroad worker and then a union leader, and had been jailed in Chicago for calling a strike. Gene was a lanky, pale man, a fiery orator, and one of the gentlest souls I ever knew. And so desperately a captive of alcohol! He had acquired the habit in his early days, and fought against it all his life. The greater a man's goals are, and the more capable his mind, the more tragic is his story when he drinks.

When Gene went on lecture tours he was accompanied by a strong man whose major duty it was to keep him fit to go on the platform. One of these men, George H. Goebel, is still living. He writes me:

> In my opinion Eugene Debs had an unusually high type of brain—so nicely adjusted that a table-spoonful of whiskey would give all the effects of a bottle. In my judgment he only got really drunk when alone, after a long strain. Twice I know, when his tour of dates had been filled, he disappeared for weeks—presumably on a batter. All over the country the reporters seemed to have an unwritten rule to say nothing of the habit, out of admiration for him.

> Yes, I traveled with Gene much of the time— had full charge of arranging the meetings after his release from Atlanta. On these tours our main difficulty was not Gene, but friends wishing to show their regard for him, trying to sneak in a bottle, although they knew we did not wish it— over and over we would confiscate it. When I say "we" I mean Otto Branstetter and Bertha Hale White. We usually had three rooms in a row, Gene in the last one—so that, with our doors open, we knew who was going by, and intercepted them.

Drink hindered and haunted them, these men like Debs; but their ideas, in those days of intellectual ferment, were a heady brew for me. I revelled in the opportunity to work and fight for the goals which were then deemed impossible and ultra-radical, and yet are now accepted as almost commonplace by the nation. Late in the summer of 1905 I sent out to everybody I knew a circular proposing an organization to teach college students the program and purposes of the Socialist movement. A dinner meeting was arranged at a restaurant on Fulton Street in New York City; some threescore men and women attended, and we organized what is now called the League for Industrial Democracy. It is still active.

I proposed Jack London as its president . . . and thus came to know the horror of his alcoholism.

London was delighted by the offer of the presidency of our new group; he notified us that he was planning to sail around Cape Horn, and would speak for us on his arrival in New York.

A mass meeting was called. Jack was at the height of his fame, and a great crowd assembled to hear him. He had landed in Florida and was coming by train, but the train was late; here was this vast crowd and no Jack London. I was asked by our group to take his place, and was panic-stricken; but I summoned my thoughts and was about to emerge on the platform when I heard a tremendous cheering, and realized that London had at last arrived. Here he came, striding up the aisle, a stocky, vigorous man just under thirty, blond-haired, the perfect Nordic type he later celebrated. He was greeted as a conquering hero, and delivered a famous speech—afterwards published in the book, *Revolution* (issued a dozen years before the Russians made that word odious). The newspapers gave his speech much space, and afterwards he went up to Yale and delivered it there.

The day after the New York meeting I sat at a luncheon

in Mouquin's restaurant with Jack and his wife, Charmian, and the editor of *Wilshire's* magazine and his wife. It was a great occasion for me, but not unmixed with sorrow—for Jack was drinking. His eyelids were inflamed, and there were in his face and speech all the signs of alcoholism I had learned to recognize. He ordered drinks throughout the meal and during the hours of talk which followed.

He chose to take my non-drinking as a challenge. Not in an angry way—and yet, as I look back with my present knowledge of psychology, I know there must have been powerful conflicts in his subconscious. He chose to tease me by reciting his prodigious exploits as a drinking man. It had all begun, he said, when he was five years old and had drunk some of a pailful of beer which he was carrying to his step-father, at work in the fields. At five, Jack London had drunk himself into insensibility!

Picture him sitting in the restaurant—blue eyes, golden hair, regular features, florid complexion, eager voice and sparkling humor, telling what he had seen and done. At the age of ten he was tramping the streets of Oakland, throwing newspapers at doorways. There was nothing especially thrilling about this, he said; but when he went into saloons, *there* he found excitement of all sorts. Men were noisy, they laughed loudly, everything was big and splendid, and sometimes there were fights. Even the drunks slumped over the tables or lying on the sawdust-covered floor seemed adventurous and glamorous. Saloons were the place where men made acquaintanceships, where they struck bargains and sealed them with a quick toss of a shot-glass.

Then, when he was fourteen, Jack was employed on a boat in the harbor. In the cabin he entered a drinking bout with two men. He took "drink for drink" with them, and the result was that the two men went under the table, while Jack, still a boy, was able to go up on deck and walk about. This made him most proud of himself; but looking back on it he decided that the more fortunate man was the one who could take only two drinks and not lose his self-control. The man who could go on drinking indefinitely was tempted to do it, and the results were far more serious in the end.

He next bought an oyster boat, and the deal was put through in Johnny Heinhold's saloon, called "The Last Chance." The money was paid, the receipt signed, and then it was up to the seller to treat to a round of drinks. Everybody in the place was invited. Everybody ordered whiskey. It was bad whiskey, but Jack "tossed it down."

Now, seated at this table in a New York restaurant, Jack London told us about the old town of Benicia, on the Carquinez Straits, the town he made the headquarters of his oyster boat. Jack had a job with the fish patrol; and both during and after hours he held his own with the most reckless of the drinkers—it was "a matter of prestige." One time when he was drunk he crawled under the nets in the drying frames, and in the morning had to be disentangled from them. It was a great joke, and he shared in it. For a period of three weeks he "never drew a sober breath," and that was the apex of glory.

He drank now at every opportunity. He made the saloons his home; he began to lose interest in food. He woke up in the morning with his fingers afflicted with palsy and his stomach feeling the same way. He had to have a whole glass of whiskey to brace him up. He tells us about a political parade in Oakland; the political bosses hired all the bums and waterfront gangsters to march, carrying torches. They got

THE CUP OF FURY 53

free liquor for it; then later they raided the bars and saloons, seized a new supply of bottles and drank until stupefied.

Next Jack London shipped out as a seal hunter. There were crazy scenes in the Bonin Islands when the crews went ashore. In a Japanese house of entertainment he sat talking and drinking with a pal. Another dropped in, then another, and each treated in turn. They hired a Japanese orchestra, and just as the *samisens* and the *taikos* started their strange melodies, there came a wild scream from the street; they recognized the voice of one of their shipmates, a sailor who was known to go berserk when drunk. This man didn't stop for a doorway—he simply burst through the paper walls of the building. His eyes were blood-shot and he was wildly waving his arms. Says Jack, describing the event: "The orchestra fled; so did we. We went through doorways, and we went through paper walls—anything to get away."

Then the wanderer came back—"Home is the sailor!"— and this is what Jack London found in his old Oakland haunts. One friend had been shot while drunk and resisting arrest, and another who had helped him was in prison. Four others were dead, another had been drowned, another was hiding up the river from the police; some were in San Quentin or Folsom, state prisons. The "King of the Greeks," who had been Jack's pal in Benicia, had fled abroad after killing two men. Another man had been stabbed through the lung.

Jack decided that he was through with the sea and the waterfront. He got a job in a steam laundry and there began "industrial drinking," the disease I later portrayed as it took place in the stockyards in Chicago. When Saturday night came, he was utterly exhausted and *wanted* to get drunk. "I, the long-time intimate of John Barleycorn, knew just what he promised me—maggots of fancy, dreams of power, forget-fulness, anything and everything save whirling washers, revolving mangles, humming centrifugal wringers, and fancy starch, and interminable processions of Dutch trousers moving in steam under my flying iron."

Such were the stories Jack told me at our restaurant table, and you can understand why I was saddened. He went away to keep his engagements, and I saw him no more on that trip.

5

THERE IS ANOTHER reason why I remember that afternoon with Jack London so vividly. At that time I was writing the last pages of a book called *The Jungle*—a novel which would soon be translated into twenty-seven languages, would eventually be read by tens of millions of people all over the world, and would change the laws and ways of America in sweeping and startling fashion.

It was this book which gave me the strange and enduring title, "King of the Muckrakers"—a phrase used as recently as a few months ago when Edward R. Murrow introduced me on his "This I Believe" radio program. It is a phrase which emboldens me now to challenge the octopus industries producing alcoholic beverages.

The Jungle brought me together with many men and women whom I eventually came to know intimately, and about whom I will speak as we go on. "Not since Byron," said one newspaper, "has there been such an example of worldwide celebrity won in a day by a book as has come to Upton Sinclair."

And so I will tell you the story of *The Jungle,* and how I came to write it.

Ever since I had stopped writing juvenile thrillers, I had been attempting to write "the great American novel." Two books failed; then I conceived of a third—a trilogy, in fact—dealing with our American Civil War. *"That the men of this land may know the heritage which has come down to them"* —so read the inscription. George D. Herron promised me thirty dollars a month so that I might write this book, and I betook myself and my family to Princeton, New Jersey, where the university library had a great Civil War collection. On a ridge three miles north of town I put up two tents.

We spent the summer in the tents, and in the fall I assisted in the building of a three-room cottage and a shack, size eight by ten, in which I did my writing. I lived in that neighborhood for four years, and met the people and listened to their talk and their gossip. It was, I decided, an enfeebled community; the vigorous elements had been moving westward through a couple of centuries. It was significant to my anti-poverty thinking that those who possessed hundred-acre farms were usually respectable and hardworking people, while the hard-put owners of five- and ten-acre farms fell prey to tuberculosis and other diseases, and frequently went off to the city to get drunk and "forget." Others stayed where they were and made apple-jack and kept themselves half-stupefied.

One such family lived down the slope below us. They had no land at all, but squatted in a ramshackle cabin. They had eight or ten half-clad children; and they drank all the hard liquor they could get. They lived, I was told, by trading horses and cows, but it was generally believed that most of these were stolen from distant places. My ducks and geese often wandered down that way to the brook, and when the flock came back at night there would be yet another one missing.

But neither such petty annoyances nor the building of shacks stayed my pen. I wrote like one possessed. And after a year there was the novel *Manassas*. It was accepted by the Macmillan Company, and Jack London called it "the best Civil War book I've read." It received good reviews, but it did not sell. Thus the total of my earnings from my first four novels was less than a thousand dollars.

However, the editor of *Appeal to Reason* read *Manassas*, and suggested that I do a similar novel dealing with present-day conditions. He offered me five hundred dollars in advance for the serial rights, and to me this was a fortune. I chose the Chicago stockyards as my subject. A great strike had just taken place in the meat industry; the unions had been crushed, and I had read a pamphlet describing the evil working conditions which existed there. So I went off to Chicago, engaging a room in the Stockyards Hotel. I spent seven weeks wandering about the Yards. My clothing was such that I could be taken for a workingman, and I found that I could go anywhere.

In "Back-of-the-Yards," I saw much of John Barleycorn. And I found the "System" described by Lincoln Steffens in full operation: the packers, the police and the saloonkeepers were allies. Their aim was to wring the last ounce of labor-power out of the workers, and then pick the last penny of slim wages out of their pockets. Wandering about on a Sunday afternoon, I saw a wedding procession entering the back room of a saloon. I went in with it and watched the proceedings. I took a seat on a bench against the wall, and sat there until late in the evening. Nobody asked me any questions or objected to my presence; perhaps they thought I was a police detective. In any event, they surely could not have guessed that I was composing in my mind the opening chapter of a novel which would change their lives and their work and their world.

They were my characters, and this wedding scene was the beginning of my story. I wrote it there in my mind; I went over every paragraph until I knew it by heart; a few weeks later when I settled down in my eight-by-ten cabin, on Christmas Day of 1904, I still knew every word of that scene, and I wrote it half-blinded by my own tears.

The stockyards workers were impoverished, bewildered foreigners, imported wholesale like cattle. They could not speak English. They neither knew nor could defend their rights. If they had a wedding party, they *had* to have it in the back room of a saloon; no other place was available to them. They certainly couldn't have it in the ramshackle houses in which they lived, for often a whole family lived crowded into one room, while the other rooms were rented out to boarders in double shifts—one family sleeping at night, the other by day.

In my view of it, the urge to drink is caused in part by ignorance and in part by bad social conditions—and by this latter phrase I mean both overwork and misery of the poor, and idleness and luxury of the rich. Now, a half century later, there are still both kinds of unfortunates in America, but the stockyards workers have strong unions and earn high pay. They are free American citizens.

The Jungle was a book of protest, written at a time when the meat-packing industry knew no laws and no limitations. It was the story of Polish and Lithuanian immigrants, herded to America to work in the slaughterhouses and stockyards of Chicago. Jurgis Rudkus, a young immigrant who came to

America with his parents and the girl he loved, was my hero; he was a strong, eager Lithuanian hoping to find wealth and happiness as an American workingman.

Instead—Jurgis was trapped in "the jungle," a pit of incredible corruption, poison and filth. Uncontrolled packers, greedy for any penny of profit, willfully sold carcasses which had been condemned by inspectors. Refuse-ridden food was approved and packed. These were the facts of the stockyards in those days; and protest by the men who worked in the slaughterhouses was economic suicide.

The Jungle was a grim book; before my story ended, Jurgis Rudkus was a broken man, ruined by the stockyards system; his children were dead; his wife was forced into prostitution, and was released only by death. How far away these things may seem to you now—and how true they were then! The book was an indictment of the economic, social, and hygienic evils of the meat-packing industry; not by any means an easy book to read, nor a pleasant one.

When the manuscript was finished, I went to New York to interview George P. Brett, president of the Macmillan Company, who said that the opening chapter was "a masterpiece." But he wanted me to cut out some of the "blood and guts" from the book; nothing so horrible had ever been published in America, he said. "Not, at least, by a respectable concern." Out of his vast publishing experience he now assured me that he could sell three times as many copies of my book if I would only consent to remove the objectionable passages. If I were unwilling to do this, his firm would be compelled to decline the book. I could not take his advice; I was determined to put the facts before the public.

I forget who the other publishers were who rejected *The Jungle*. There were five in all; and by the time the last said "No," I decided to publish it myself. The editor of *Appeal to Reason* generously consented to give space to a statement of my troubles. Jack London wrote a rousing manifesto, calling on the working people to rally to the book, which he called "the 'Uncle Tom's Cabin' of wage-slavery." His comments on the manuscript added, "It is alive and warm. It is brutal with life. It is written of sweat and blood, and groans and tears." In my statement I offered a "Sustainer's Edition," price $1.20 postpaid, and in a month or two I took in $4,000 —more money than I had been able to earn in all the past five years.

In this case, the first thing I did was to buy a saddle-horse for $125. The horse could also be driven to the buggy —I had to have some form of exercise, to help the poor stomach that apparently was not equal to keeping up with the head. Also I had to have some way to get into town quickly, because now I had a business on my hands, and had to be sending telegrams and mailing proofs. I put a printing firm in New York at work setting *The Jungle* in type. Then, just as the work was completed, some one suggested that I offer the book to Doubleday, Page and Company. They accepted the novel subject to proof by an "independent report" that my scorching condemnation of the industry was true.

The "independent report" was soon ready; prepared by a newspaperman who later turned out to be a publicity man for the meat-packing industry, it declared that my book was completely inaccurate and untruthful. Doubleday checked further, learned of this frame-up, and moved ahead boldly with their publishing plans.

Then a series of articles appeared in the *Saturday Evening Post*, insisting that the packers were noble in all their motives, and that their products were free from every blemish. I read this pap, and was boiling mad; I took the first train to New

York, and sped to *Everybody's* magazine, which had just electrified the country with an exposure of Wall Street stock-juggling and stock-watering. And before their entire staff of editors, I read an 8,000-word reply to the *Saturday Evening Post* series.

It was dynamite, no mistake. In my possession I had affidavits from a wild, one-eyed Irishman who had been a foreman at the stockyards. He told under oath how condemned carcasses, thrown into the tanks to be destroyed, were surreptitiously taken out at the bottom of the tanks and sold to the city for meat! A second affidavit told how he had been offered and had accepted a $5,000.00 bribe to retract his story. The editors listened, and bought my article on the spot.

We all expected the story to blow off the roof. And it might have, except for the fact that the magazine came out the day after earthquake and fire destroyed the city of San Francisco. So no news stories went out on the condemned-meat article.

But *The Jungle* did make the first page soon after, thanks to the efforts of the greatest publicity man of that time, President Theodore Roosevelt. Roosevelt called me to Washington to discuss the meat-packers. "I bear no love for these gentlemen," he told me, "for I saw the meat they canned for the army in Cuba, and I'd as soon have eaten my old hat."

Roosevelt appointed a commission to investigate the stockyards; their report, published under pressure from the New York *Times*, proved practically every word in my book. The nation went wild with fury; the book became a best-seller; and I gave interviews and wrote statements for the press until I was dizzy.

I had at last written "the great American novel!" *The*

Jungle was a bestseller in America and in Great Britain. Photographers and reporters journeyed to Princeton, hired vehicles there and drove out to my farm; neighbors who had been selling rusty machinery and broken-down mules to me suddenly discovered that I had "put them on the map." Editors wrote or telegraphed commissions, and I was free to name my own price. The book was translated into one language after another, and my fame was worldwide.

How did it feel to be famous? I can truly say that I experienced few thrills. I wanted to take the first train to the wilderness and never come back to crowds and excitement. But "fame" did mean that newspapers and magazines would print a little bit of what I wanted to say, and that by this means hard-working men in the giant industries of America, unorganized in those days, would hear words of encouragement. And it did mean that American people, including our soldiers, would never again have to eat spoiled or diseased meat. Pure food laws with teeth in them were forced through Congress.

Nevertheless, I became impatient for new activities.

Princeton did not seem a satisfactory place in which to live. The roads were bad, my farm remote, and I had little affection for most of my neighbors. I had been reading and thinking about a co-operative home, and I invited others to join in the experiment.

I invested the money from *The Jungle* in a building, formerly a private school, on the Palisades; it was directly across the Hudson River from upper Manhattan. Including members and employees, we had some forty or fifty persons in our "co-op." Fourteen of them were children, and we achieved great success in our experiment in co-operative care by the mothers.

Here in Helicon Home Colony we had privacy in our

separate rooms, to which no one came except by invitation; and in addition, there were also common rooms. The main one had a big, four-sided fireplace about which we gathered for conversation, and such eminent persons as John Dewey and William James came here to discuss their ideas with us.

One person in our midst was destined to become eminent, although we did not know it. We kept him busy tending our furnace, sweeping our public rooms and staircases, and cleaning the little fishpond in our glass-roofed court.

His name was Harry Sinclair Lewis.

6

WE CALLED HIM Hal. He was tall and lanky, a twenty-year-old eaglet who was fledging his feathers; he had vivid red hair, and an abnormally florid complexion. You know him as Sinclair Lewis—author of *Main Street, Babbitt, Arrowsmith, Dodsworth,* and a dozen other novels.

Hal was eager, talkative, and a good listener. And at Helicon Hall, there were many people worth listening to: a philosopher from Columbia University, William P. Montague; a professor of manual arts from Teachers College; a Swedish writer, Edwin Björkman, who was translating Strindberg; a couple of minor novelists; a physician; and others who could tell much about life and letters.

Hal had quit Yale in order to learn about co-operative living. With him came a friend, Allen Updegraff, who also aspired to write. I had a secretary, Edith Summers; and these three—Hal, "Up," and Edie—formed our junior literary section. They liked to sit apart and talk about the books they read; and they spoke with zest of the books they hoped some-day to write.

Edith eventually married a workingman named Kelley, and tried raising tobacco in Kentucky; what she got out of it was starvation, and a powerful, realistic but little-read novel called *Weeds*. Later she became blind.

"Up" went to live in France, and there wrote novels, one of them giving an appalling picture of the drunkenness of American expatriates on the Riviera.

As to Hal, I have more to relate. He soon had enough of furnace-work and general education, and went off to New York. There, incidentally, he wrote a playful article about our Helicon "home-colony" life for the New York *Sun*. It has been reprinted in the collection of Hal's miscellaneous writings called *The Man From Main Street: A Sinclair Lewis Reader*, and you may enjoy reading it. It was a harmless enough piece, but it worried Professor Montague because he was teaching in a woman's college then headed by a strict lady dean; and she was not the sort to enjoy reading about her professor dancing with our pretty Irish waitress on Satur-day evenings. Particularly since Hal neglected to mention that Montague's wife, a medical student, was always present at such times! Rereading the article recently, I wondered about one thing: why young Sinclair Lewis had endowed us with a bowling alley and a swimming pool, neither of which we possessed—unless you counted the fishpond, about eight inches deep and six feet by three in area!

Years passed before I saw Sinclair Lewis again. He had become editorial adviser to a publishing house, and I offered them one of my novels, *Sylvia*. We met for lunch and Hal had the sad duty of telling me that the novel was declined. Then when I moved to California, he came to my home for an evening, bringing his first wife. More years passed, and I next saw him at his New York hotel. We corresponded sporadically, and sent each other our books. Several of mine he praised, and I quoted his opinions; and I did the same for him. On a dust-jacket recently, I saw what I wrote about *Babbitt* when it was first issued: "I am now ready to get out in the middle of the street and shout hurrah, for America's most popular novelist has sent me a copy of his new book, *Babbitt*. I am here to enter my prediction that it will be the most talked-about and the most-read novel published in this country in my lifetime."

In *Money Writes,* however, I criticized Hal's novels for lack of social vision, and this annoyed him; he never took criticism kindly, and he wrote me a cross letter. But I was told by a friend that in a group where my numerous faults were under discussion, Hal was generous enough to add as a postscript: "But you can't help liking Upton!"

I was glad of all the success that came to Lewis, and deeply regretful for the misery. For it was as in the case of Jack London: alcohol destroyed him.

I began to hear about it, but there was nothing I could do; Hal always resented any effort to interfere. I met an oldtime journalist with an absorbingly interesting story of real life to tell, and I said to him, "You ought to get Sinclair Lewis to help you make that into a bestseller." His answer was, "No, thank you! He is doing his writing on booze. He gets drunk in public and makes violent rows, and I'm too good a quarreler myself." More details came from the writer William E. Woodward. Bill told me that never had he seen anyone get so blind drunk as "Red" Lewis. He had been drunk in Woodward's home for days and nights.

The art expert, Martin Birnbaum—who was my classmate in college—tells of an excursion out of Venice on a yacht owned by the Princess Marina Raspoli. "We suddenly missed 'Red,' and when we found him, he was so hilariously drunk that we had to ship him back to Venice." Martin's nephew, the late Dr. Jerome Ziegler, "was the only man who could control [Lewis] when he was seized with a desire to drink." Phyllis Bottome, who was a close friend, attributes his mad drinking to his two marriage failures. She calls his first "a most heart-rending senseless marriage," and his second "bitingly unsuccessful."

My own belief is that drinking is a cause rather than a result of marriage failure; but I suppose it is like the problem of the hen and the egg—each is both cause and effect. Phyllis pays tribute to "his peculiar powers of sympathy and kindness. I think," she says, "that he would have done anything for his friends, and at any sacrifice; and I think that any man was his friend who treated him with integrity and good feeling." This I can confirm.

For some of his doings—such as getting slapped by Theodore Dreiser, or for standing in a church pulpit and "daring" God to prove that He existed by striking him dead on the spot—I used to get some of the blame. The similarity in our names caused confusion in people's minds.

I would receive his mail and he would get mine. In 1935 my wife and I took a twenty-thousand-mile motor tour, while I lectured in thirty or forty cities. In St. Louis I had as chairman an eminent astronomer, and he spoke as follows: "Ladies and gentlemen, when I consented to introduce the speaker of this evening I made a study of his life and works and wrote a paper which I asked my son to read and revise for me. My son informed me that I had got hold of the wrong writer; that our speaker was *not* the author of *Main Street* and *Babbitt*. So I made another study and wrote another paper, which my son has approved." The astronomer then read a brief account of my life and works, and concluded: "And now, ladies and gentlemen, I take great pleasure in introducing *Mr. Sinclair Lewis!*"

The facts concerning our ex-furnaceman's misfortune have been revealed in biographical material which appeared after his death—the quart of brandy a day, the shakes, the tapering off, the swearing off, the wine phase, the wandering over the earth, the avoiding of friends and the seeking for peace where there is no peace, the decline in writing power, and the final delirium.

Hal wrote his last novel in Europe. His closest friend at the time was Perry Miller, professor of American literature at Harvard University; and in the April, 1951, issue of *The Atlantic Monthly,* Dr. Miller compassionately described his friend's final months in these words:

As soon as he finished the manuscript, he started drinking, until his Florentine physician forbade him spirits. When I reached him in April, he was guzzling quantities of red wine, and despite Aleck's strenuous efforts, he generally succeeded in knocking himself out by afternoon. *(Editor's note: Alexander Manson was "secretary, chauffeur, nurse, and interpreter" to Lewis during the last months of his life.)* At a Florentine restaurant he commanded the orchestra to play the sentimental tunes of his earlier escapades; he peeled off and flung about five-thousand-lira notes—Babbitt on a spree—until Aleck could get him out and pour him into the car. By August he was drinking only beer, but he had already had two serious heart attacks and should not have touched even that.

I suppose hundreds of people in three decades have seen Sinclair Lewis drunk; no doubt he made a vast public spectacle of himself. I cannot say what kept him going through the years of creativity; I do know that at the end of it, his back to the wall, facing himself drunk or sober, he did not flinch. There was something positively reckless about it. He was not drinking because he was miserable and wanted solace; neither was he what you would call a drunkard. He was no disenchanted, alcoholic Scott Fitzgerald, drinking compulsively. There may not have been much joy in what Red was doing, but there was still plenty of defiance.

Through a miracle of physical stamina, Hal made it to the age of sixty-six. More tragic than any shortage of years was the loss of productivity, the absence of joy. He must have suffered in those last days in Rome, waiting for death to take him out of the clutches of his tormentor.

Catastrophe struck Helicon Home Colony a couple of months after Hal had left for New York.

At four o'clock on a Sunday morning in March I was awakened by thundering crashes. To get out of the tower room where I slept, I had to run along an open balcony to the stairway. The place was afire; heated air was blowing out of the stucco walls of the building. Flames swept up over the balcony, and I remember how they scorched my nightshirt and one side of my head. I ran across the open court, over embers and broken glass, and we all shouted alarms and searched for anyone who may have been trapped.

The place burned to the ground. And one life was lost.

No liquor had ever been served at the Helicon Home Colony, and I doubt that any was ever brought to the rooms. Except this once.

A carpenter had been employed temporarily, and he slept in an upper-story room. I was told afterwards that he had been drinking heavily the night before; the calls, the crashing sounds, the shouting never penetrated his stupor.

He, poor man — like so many people I've known — had been drinking the night before because it made him feel "gay" and "high" and "good."

7

I HAD BEEN corresponding with George Sterling regularly during all these years. We had not met; but our letters were warm and wide-ranging and stimulating. And from Jack London I had learned much about the California poet.

I learned that Jack left his manuscripts with George when he went off to sea; that at such times he gave George full authority to edit and market them. Even more: George was authorized to do "ghost writing" when and if he needed money; he had Jack's permission to write stories, sign the famous London name to them, and then sell them at the high prices Jack's by-line could command. Friendship could go no further. Indeed, I think it should not have gone so far! But George knew Jack's ideas and style, and he was not the sort to abuse a friendship or take advantage of a kindness.

I remember a photograph of Sterling which Jack once showed me. George stood as erect as an Indian, and had the body of an athlete. His profile bore a startling resemblance to Doré's profile of Dante.

George lived in Carmel, California. It was then a small village; it had — and still has! — a greater variety of scenic beauty than any other place I know. There is the broad Pacific . . . a sandy beach . . . and a rocky point with windswept cypress trees. The village sits in a pine forest; at one side is a fertile valley, and behind is a semi-circle of mountains.

George suggested in a letter that I visit Carmel. The pace of the past several months had been furious. After the disaster at Helicon, I had worked on three, perhaps four novels. I had worked in New York and then in Bermuda; I had overworked. And then came the news of my father's lonely death in a hospital ward.

I decided to make the trip to California. George lived in a little bungalow with his wife, Carrie, and he borrowed for my use a cottage belonging to Arnold Genthe, the art photographer.

Across the bay from us in Oakland was the Ruskin Club, organized by the city's librarian. The members announced a dinner at which I would be "welcomed" to California's literary community; and, of course, George was to write and read a poem marking the occasion.

We took a train from Carmel to San Francisco, arriving in the afternoon; and because there was time to spare, our first stop was the Bohemian Club. George was an honored member, their poet laureate. They held a room for him, rent free. And he was the author of a masque for their annual "hi-jinks," held in the summer in the redwood groves.

My host guided me to the Bohemian Club bar. The moment he appeared, one of the members came forward and sought the "honor" of buying us a drink. Then another man joined us, and he too had to buy drinks. And then the first had to reciprocate with yet another round; and so it went. And as I sat there, sipping thin lemonade, I wondered how — even if they could drink it without effect — they had so much room for so much whiskey!

Then, much later, we took the cable car down to the ferry which crossed the waters between San Francisco and Oakland. Standing on the front deck of the boat, looking out over the harbor, George showed me the wavering, rainbow-colored circles of light riding on the water, caused by thin slicks of oil. He explained that these had been the source of his inspiration for *The Wine of Wizardry*. He was talking rapidly; his sentences flamed with magnificent, glowing imagery; yet almost none of it was coherent. It was as though Sterling were repeating the phrases of a great poem, but speaking them out of their proper order, and with no logical connecting words between each phrase. I was puzzled, and tried my best to understand what he meant, and couldn't imagine what was the matter with me. Finally it dawned upon me that my friend and host was drunk. Before we got to the banquet hall, an acquaintance took him off to be walked around the block to try to "work it off." But George did not reappear; someone else had to read his poem for him.

He came to my cottage the next day in that state of humiliation which is so painful in the drinker. And with him came a flood of memories of the full, frustrating quarter of a century I had spent taking care of my father; I was resolved to have no more of drinkers. We spoke, and I told George I was planning to leave. Tears came to his eyes, and he said, "Upton, I give you my word of honor: if you will stay I will not touch another drop of liquor while you are here." I stayed on at Carmel as long as possible, and George kept his word.

I remember one day: we got buckets full of abalone, those sea creatures with one curved shell which cling to the rocks deep under the water. At low tide you dive and pry them off with a steel hook. They were cooked into a delicious stew, and all George's friends, the writers and painters of Carmel, assembled for a party. George had written "The Abalone Song," and a decade of poets exercised their wits in finding rhymes for the word "abalone" — bony, stony, groany, macaroni, and so on. Many brought liquor, but George remained a sober man at the feast.

A school of poets centered about San Francisco, and George knew them all. He told me about a revered older poet, Ina Coolbrith, who had befriended Jack London when he was a boy; and about Nora May French, a young girl who had written lovely verses, but who later committed suicide by jumping off the cliff at Point Lobos. George was sensitive and reticent on the subject, and did not tell me the reason; others, however, described how she had become an early slave to drink.

Another poet who lived nearby was Joaquin Miller, whose home was on the heights above Oakland; he proudly, punningly called himself "the Poet Lariat of the Sierras." Miller was the author of a famous poem about Columbus, which perhaps you have read in one of your school books. It is in most of them: "Sail on! Sail on!" A drinking man, Miller had spent his early years in the "doggeries" of San Francisco. Then he took his verses to England, where he wore a sombrero and chaps and highheeled boots with spurs, and made an immense impression on the aristocracy by smoking two cigars at once. He was "the real Wild West," he told them. Now he was a patriarch with flowing white whiskers, talking about his past and announcing that the source of his inspiration was whiskey.

Another local writer with a drinking history was Ambrose Bierce. Friends told me it was Bierce who was responsible for George's weakness. George had been educated in a Catholic school on Long Island, and had been a pupil and friend of Father Tabb, the poet. When he arrived in California to work for his rich uncle, Bierce met him — and, at his most sensitive age, led George into reckless drinking. Bierce was a brilliant writer, and described himself as "an eminent tankardman." His tongue was ferocious, and his hatreds deep; he had allied himself with my traditional opponents, the Hearst newspapers, and had chosen me as one of his targets. In fact, he broke with both George Sterling and Jack London because they remained my friends.

A prolific author, his collected works fill twelve full volumes. His war stories were realistic and noteworthy; his philosophies were destructive. In *The Devil's Dictionary*, one of the most acid books ever written, he delighted in definitions such as this:

"HAPPINESS — an agreeable sensation arising from contemplating the misery of another."

Bierce was portrayed in these words by a fellow-cynic, Henry Mencken:

"There was nothing of the milk of kindness in old Ambrose; he did not get the nickname of Bitter Bierce for nothing. What delighted him most in this life was the spectacle of human cowardice and folly. He put man, intellectually, somewhere between the sheep and the horned cattle, and as a hero somewhere below the rats. . . So far in this life, indeed, I have encountered no more thorough-going cynic than Bierce was."

Bierce filled the voids in his world by drinking; yet his amazing constitution carried him into his seventieth year — a most unhappy one. He had reached that stage of alcoholism where it is torment to be alive. And in this period of anguish, he selected a strange way to end his life: he wandered off into Mexico, then aflame with war and banditry, and died in a manner unreported and still unknown. "There — if legend is to be believed," says Mencken, "he marched into the revolution then going on, and had himself shot..."

This, then, was the atmosphere in which George Sterling fought hopelessly and helplessly against alcohol; the setting in which Jack London had determined to drink "skillfully and discreetly"; the world in which Carrie Sterling, George's wife, struggled in a web of doom. I have a photograph of these three, sailing on a boat in San Francisco bay; it is a lovely picture of three handsome, talented, youthful people. Think: all three of them were to take their own lives!

It was long after I left Carmel. I had gone back to work — in Greenwich Village, in Florida, in Alabama, in Europe. I had visited England and Holland, Paris and London, and spent magnificent hours with Romain Rolland, George Bernard Shaw, Frederik van Eeden, and H. G. Wells.

And then I returned to New York City. George Sterling was there. And there, too, was a young lady from Mississippi. I have much to tell you about this lady, who later became my wife and has been my wife for forty-three years. I think most highly of her, although I am not encouraged to say so in public. She has no vanity in her makeup, and shuns publicity.

Her name was Mary Craig Kimbrough, and she was born in the Delta district of Mississippi, where there were nine Negroes to each white. She has endless stories to tell about these primitive black folk and the white land-owners who continued, even after the Civil War, to act as their "masters." She discovered that the sophisticates of New York and Europe would leave all other topics to gather around and listen to her tales. They had read much the same sort of thing in a hundred romances, and called it sentimental and passé. But here it was, come to life in the person of one young woman. Moonlight and star-jessamine. Live oaks with Spanish moss hanging from giant branches. Real Negro mammies and former slaves. Beaus coming on horseback, and serenades under the windows, with Negro bands playing the music they heard drifting out from the "white folks'" pianos — and changing this music into a new idiom. And while the black men played, young white serenaders capered and danced on the lawn below the windows of the "big house." There were stately balls in Craig's home, opening with the "grand march" and lasting until dawn. On one such occasion a fire started in the second story of a mansion, and it was impossible to put it out; and so the young people went on dancing until the roof began to cave in. Suitors from everywhere came bringing bouquets; one young man outdid the others by coming to call with a servant behind "toting" a whole tree in blossom. Another brought Craig a live wildcat he had captured. This ferocious creature broke loose in the house, causing pandemonium.

Craig's father was a planter, a bank president, and later a judge. She had six tall brothers and two sisters, all younger than herself, and she had taken care of them while her mother toured the state, campaigning first for a home for Confederate veterans, and second against the dire threat of "woman suffrage." Craig tells a story about her mother: the Judge came home hungry one evening, and "Aunt" Catherine, ex-slave and a marvelous cook, informed him that there was no dinner to serve. "Miss Ma'y ain't tole me what to have," Catherine explained. The Judge tip-toed up to the attic where Miss Ma'y had locked herself in; and when he tapped on the door, her response was, "Go away and be quiet! I am writing an article on 'Woman the Homemaker'."

Craig attended Mississippi State College for Women, and then a finishing school on Fifth Avenue in New York. She later returned to that school with a younger sister, and there had as private tutor in literature a young instructor from Columbia named Clayton Hamilton. Hamilton told Craig that she could write, and so she had gone back home and at her mother's urging had written a book with a florid title, *The Queen of a Mystic Court.* Her subject was Winnie Davis, "the daughter of the Confederacy." Judge Kimbrough had been a friend of the Jefferson Davis family, and executor of what was left of the estate; and Craig's family had all the letters concerning a very touching story of the Confederacy. Craig could write that story as no one else, for she had herself been so very much a "Southern belle."

At the age of seventeen, a lovely creature with red-gold hair, and eyes to match, Craig became engaged to a young man of her county. The two fathers were the wealthiest in the community. The match was considered perfect, except that the boy was what in the South they call "wild." He drank; and Craig's father wisely insisted upon a long engagement. Then a year later the Judge came to Craig and told her she must break off the engagement. She had never disobeyed him in her life, and never thought of doing so now. Broken-hearted, she was sent off to spend the winter in Virginia, while the boy went off to New Orleans on a long spree. A few years later, he took his own life.

To Craig many new suitors presented themselves. Her mother pleaded on behalf of one of them, but in vain; Craig was certain that she would never marry, nor let herself fall in love again.

In one aspect, her life paralleled mine. In my case it was my father and uncles who drank; and in her case it was not only the man she had hoped to marry, but also — much earlier — a favorite uncle, her mother's brother. He bore an honored name; he was a lineal descendant of the English noblewoman, Lady Southworth, who had come to Massachusetts and married the first colonial governor.

Craig's uncle was a man who owned two plantations; a handsome man with elegant manners and a kind heart. A man who grieved over the fate of the black people, their ignorance and their sufferings, and grieved over the larger problem of racial inequality — for which, however, he could see no solution. But he was nevertheless a man with nothing to do: his managers ran the two plantations. He would "drown his sorrow" in drink, and there were those in town who encouraged him to drink and then gambled with him. He sometimes gambled away half the income from a plantation in a single night, and all such debts he considered debts of honor.

The person he loved best, next to his wife, was his little niece, Mary Craig Kimbrough; and she alone could handle him when he drank. Someone in town would come by to say that he was in trouble. A plantation hand would hitch up a horse, and Craig would drive into town. She would find her uncle and beg him to come home, and he would make excuses and try to evade her; but when she insisted, he would meekly climb into the carriage. And then at home the women of the family would go through that sad sobering-up routine which my mother and I had learned so well.

This had gone on all through Craig's childhood. One time when they were trying to keep liquor away from him, he remembered a cask of brandied peaches aging in the cellar. He bored a little hole in it and sucked the brandy out with a straw. This kind of thing went on and grew worse — until at last the wretched man took poison. His dead body was brought to Craig's home, and it was her duty to sit with her aunt all night, while the bereaved woman lay moaning, over and over and over, "Oh, my poor thing! My poor thing!"

Craig journeyed to New York with the Winnie Davis manuscript, seeking a publisher. She had shed her tears and had begun to think. She was anxious to meet the giants of the literary world, sure that these people would have answers to her questions. She was staying in the home of friends, and was told that a famous California poet was coming for a visit — George Sterling. He was alone, now, estranged from Carrie. And he was attracted to Craig as though drawn by a magnet. She did not reciprocate his feelings, but enjoyed talking with him and hearing his ideas. I sometimes joined in these sprightly hours of conversation.

One day during the period when Craig was revising the Winnie Davis manuscript, she was walking on Riverside Drive with George Sterling. I happened along, and I exclaimed in my usual tactless, talk-first-and-think-afterwards fashion: "You don't look well, Craig. So thin — you look like a skull!"

They walked on; the poet was exasperated, and exclaimed, "Really — I'm going to kill that man someday!" But Craig only laughed and said, "He's the first man who ever told me the truth. I believe I will marry him." She

said it partly as a jest; it was the way she had been taught
—to tease men, to make disconcerting remarks, to throw
them off balance and cause them to reveal their true
character. But what she really meant was that she was tired
of flattery.

We are all determined by our temperaments. Craig was
certain to prefer the social reformer over the art-for-art's-
sake poet. Also, she had come to know John Barleycorn and
all his seasons and stratagems, and she would give her preference to the man who turned down his wine glass at a
dinner party. When it came my turn to walk with her on
Riverside Drive, she was amused but not too troubled to
observe that I had put on my "Sunday best" gloves in her
honor — but at the same time was wearing tennis shoes!

Forty-three years later she still laughs at my usually-
laughable clothes.

8

Our first home was a little cottage which stood on the edge of a woodland on the outskirts of Croton, New York. Clement Wood, a poet, served as my secretary. Another poet, Frank Shay, could usually be found washing dishes at the sink, his eyes riveted on a propped-up book. George Sterling used to come to visit us, and chopped down some chestnut trees and cut them up for the fireplace. George was "on the water-wagon" then; he was serene and lovable.

Nearby in Croton was a large house on a little hill, and in it lived the sister of Isadora Duncan, and a troupe of their adopted children in training as dancers. In peaceful, pleasant Croton, that home was perhaps the loveliest of all places to visit. Floyd Dell, who also lived nearby, was led to write a sonnet which began with these lines:

Is this the morning of the world, and these
Stars from the burning hand of God outflung?

I had met Isadora in New York and had seen her dancing on the stage of Carnegie Hall. It was like no other dancing seen before or since, and I lack words to describe its supernal beauty. Isadora danced the great music of Beethoven, Tchaikowsky and Chopin. She danced the great emotions of freedom, love, grief and revolt. One thing I hold against the motion-picture industry is that it made no permanent record of the unequalled art of Isadora Duncan.

Yet concerning this great soul I came to possess frightening knowledge. She became a dipsomaniac, struggling in vain against the need to drink. Three tragedies in her life sent her again and again to the momentary forgetfulness of alcohol. First, the death of her two children — Deirdre and Patrick, along with their nurse — in an automobile accident in Paris. Next, the loss of a hoped-for child — the baby was born dead. And then the ironic happening when she went to Greece under the patronage of the King to revive the ancient art of the dance. She brought her famed troupe of adopted children with her; one of them had grown mature and beautiful. And the man whom Isadora loved fell in love with this young girl.

As she tells the story: "While I endeavored to teach my pupils Beauty, Calm, Philosophy, and Harmony, I was inwardly writhing in the clutch of most deadly torment. ...The only resource I had was to assume an armor of exaggerative gaiety and try to drown my sufferings in the heady wines of Greece every night that we supped by the sea. There might certainly have been a nobler way, but I was not then capable of finding it."

Alas, she never did find it. Max Eastman, who knew her well, told me that her drinking was "insane"; and she died in an accident which was surely as insane as it was needless. Isadora went for an automobile ride with a scarf wrapped around her neck; a scarf so long that it fluttered in the wind. It was long enough to get caught in a whirling wheel of the car. The scarf jerked tight and snapped her neck.

Isadora Duncan never achieved the fame in her own country which was accorded her abroad. Acclaimed in London, Paris, Berlin, Athens and Moscow, she was received coldly in our major cities. In New York's Greenwich Village, a cult of young dancers and artists recognized her immortal talents; but in this same small area of New York, where so many brilliant minds were at work, the code of the "Flaming Twenties" had already become ingrained. And people hurtled from enthusiasm to enthusiasm, from idol to idol.

In the old days, Greenwich Village had been a center of fashion and wealth; then, after the turn of the century, many of the fine old mansions were converted into boarding-houses. Others were transformed into dark and dismal lodgings with tiny shops on the ground floors, and even tinier apartments above. The area was discovered by writers, artists and musicians who wanted to live as cheaply as possible and "do what they pleased." Young radicals came to the area; the Village became the battleground of the right-wing Socialists and the left-wing Socialists, the right-wing Communists and the left-wing Communists, and a few anarchists. Here, in short, was post-war ferment — bubbling, explosive, intoxicating and intoxicated.

The young people of the Village were milling about

blindly, seeking pleasure and trampling one another. Their credo was stated in the lines of two brief poems.

The substance of the first was this: Because she loved you on Wednesday, you must not expect that she will therefore love you on Thursday.

I quote the second:

> *My candle burns at both ends;* X
> *It will not last the night;*
> *But ah, my foes, and oh, my friends—*
> *It gives a lovely light.*

I have forgotten when and where I met Edna St. Vincent Millay, who wrote these verses. But no one who knew her can forget her vivid, charming personality. Everybody loved Edna; she set the tempo of the time; she served as a minstrel for the madness.

Phyllis Bottome, who knew her intimately, says in a letter: "Edna was a very strange character... At nineteen, you may remember, she won the Pulitzer Prize for her poems; and when I first knew her, considerably later on in her late twenties in Europe, she was already very spoiled; but she did not drink then, and I think only began to some years after her marriage."

I will tell you of a few of the people who "burned their candles at both ends" — people whom I first came to know in Greenwich Village. Some, like Edna, worked on for many years, writing and lecturing and aware of the changes in the world. Others "gave a lovely light" ever so briefly. Others died so miserably that it is hard to remember that they were once loved and applauded.

One of the shining stars of the Greenwich Village galaxy in the Twenties was Maxwell Bodenheim. He wrote "imagistic poetry," and highly-spiced novels with such titles as *Replenishing Jessica, Naked on Roller Skates,* and *Crazy Man.* As the most Bohemian of the many Bohemians who lived and worked in the Village, Bodenheim enjoyed a great vogue; his books were bestsellers, and money was no problem. Beautiful young women pursued him. He lived in an alcoholic glory.

What follows, however, sounds like an old-fashioned moralistic story out of those bound volumes of the *Christian Herald* which I read as a child in the home of my Methodist grandfather. "Bodey" became a miserable bum. He picked up a few coins here and there by posing as a blind man; at other times, he slumped over tables in Village bars, offering to write "poetry" for tourists who would buy him a drink.

Here is the rest of the story, as the New York *Times* told it on February 8, 1954:

Maxwell Bodenheim, the personification of Greenwich Village and Bohemia of the nineteen twenties, was found murdered with his wife yesterday in a dingy fifth-floor furnished room on the fringes of the Bowery . . . The aging, unkempt writer was lying on his back on the floor of the unheated, five-dollar-a-week room. His attractive, dark-haired wife lay on the room's single cot. On a small table nearby were copies of scribbled poems, a pad of paper and pencils, and an empty liquor bottle.

"The motive was not robbery," Chief of Detectives Thomas Nielson said. Friends of the poet said they believe the slaying might have been the result of a drinking dispute. . .

For the last few years Mr. Bodenheim had been a pathetic and ineffectual figure, wandering through the streets of the Village and the Bowery.

But in the nineteen twenties and thirties he was one of the most spectacular and controversial as well as one of the most eccentric of the country's young writers.

He was the laureate of Bohemia, and a fabulous literary scapegrace. His was the era of bathtub gin, long-haired poets, and bobbed-haired women; of all-night drinking bouts, free love, and intellectual anarchism.

...A handsome and striking man in his youth, Mr. Bodenheim was always surrounded by feminine admirers. In 1928 he was involved in a series of scandals when one of these committed suicide, a second attempted suicide, and a third died in a railway wreck...

In the nineteen thirties, when his books and his poems stopped selling, Mr. Bodenheim slipped into the poverty that marked the rest of his life. For a while he was on relief. In 1935 when he was reported dying from tuberculosis, Greenwich Village poets and painters organized a fund drive to send him to the West. They raised $12, and he stayed in New York...

George Cram Cook was another luminary of the Greenwich Village literary scene. The author of *The Chasm*, a novel which I admired greatly, George played a major part in many of New York City's cultural activities. He and his wife, Susan Glaspell, organized the Playwrights' Theatre in 1915; earlier, he had founded the Provincetown Players on Cape Cod, in "an old fish-house which Mrs. Wilbur Daniel Steele had taken for a studio, at the end of Mary Heaton Vorse's wharf." If you want an unusual picture of George — or "Jig," as we called him — read Floyd Dell's novel of the "lost generation," *Moon-calf*. Jig was the model for Tom Alden in that novel.

Cook was the discoverer of Eugene O'Neill. He was applauded as a poet, playwright, and novelist; and then, suddenly, he disappeared from the scene, and the next we heard he and Susan had gone to live in Greece.

Jig died there, and Susan later told his story in a book called *The Road to the Temple*. In it she took what seems to me to be a singular view of her husband's heavy drinking. She wrote:

> All his life this man had a habit of occasion-ally getting drunk and seeing truth from a new plane. He saw then, saw what was pretending, in himself, and others. It would begin in good times with friends — self-consciousness and timid-ities going down in the warmth of sympathetic drinking. There was a sublimated playfulness, ideas became a great game, and in play with them something that had not been before came into being.

And then she quotes her husband's own comments on drinking. Some people, he said, "drink only with their bellies. But true drinking is an affair of the head and heart. There must be a second, finer ferment in the mind — a brewing and refining of raw wit and wisdom."

Now again it is Jig's wife who is speaking. "Long afterwards," she says, "he had what I venture to call a somewhat God-like relation of wine and vision. Drinking was one of the things in which Jig succeeded, in which he realized himself as human being and artist. Yet he saw the black thing it may become."

Yes, he saw it — but apparently his wife did not. Jig

had been filled with dreams of the classic glory of Greece. He yearned to the peasant life of Greece as a child seeking the pot of gold at the foot of the rainbow. They had left America and travelled three thousand miles to fulfill this hope of his life. And at last they reached the mountain near Delphi where the two summits of Parnassus reach to the sky. One of these summits is consecrated to Apollo and to the Muses, the nine daughters of Zeus who preside over poetry, song, the arts and sciences. The other summit is sacred to Bacchus, the god of wine. "To climb Parnassus" is to write golden poetry. Just to see it, to stand before it, had been the dream of George Cram Cook.

And what did he say after peering up at Parnassus? His wife quotes his words: "Well, come on, let's go some place and have a drink."

"Next day," she continues in her book, "was one of those times of particular beauty in our household. 'Hangover days' we called them, and they have a subtle, fragile, sensitive quality. Satisfied by a violent encounter with life, one has a rarefied sense of being something nearer pure spirit. These are isolated days, no use trying to go on with things. Perhaps not so isolated as suspended. A woman who has never lived with a man who sometimes 'drinks to excess' has missed one of the satisfactions that is like a gift — taking care of the man she loves when he has had this sweetness as of a new-born soul."

My comments on these passages from Susan Glaspell's book appeared in a volume I wrote, titled *Money Writes*. They were as follows:

I cannot recall ever having read a greater piece of nonsense from the pen of a modern emancipated woman. The plain truth, which stares at us between every line of the closing narrative, is that poor Jig Cook, a poet who pinned his faith on Bacchus instead of Minerva, was at the age of fifty a pitiful, white-haired sot... dead to the whole modern world, wandering about lost among ragged peasants. He died of an infection utterly mysterious to his wife — who apparently knows nothing of the effects of alcohol.

It seems to me now that unwittingly, innocently, a husband or wife can help John Barleycorn in his almost inevitable march to victory. The "good" mate does not nag; she mixes the cocktail, she proffers the flask. The "good" spouse does not make a scene; he sits silent as another round is ordered, as another bottle is drained. There are other ways — but so often the easy way seems the "best" way.

I thought of this when Edna St. Vincent Millay came to Pasadena in 1940 on a lecture tour. I greeted her in a dressing room of the Pasadena Community Theatre, and we sat down to chat. With her was her husband, Eugen Boissevain, a Dutch importer. I had met him years before in Greenwich Village; he was a charming, kind fellow who had previously been married to Inez Milholland, the suffrage worker. When it came time for Edna to go on stage and speak, Eugen drew a flask from his back pocket and handed it to his wife. She took a heavy swig. Nothing was said; evidently, this was routine.

I went out and listened while she read a dozen or more of her poems to an audience of ladies; then when it was over, I went behind the scenes again; and there Eugen produced the flask again, and I watched Edna empty it.

I know that people use alcohol to "relieve their tensions." The Premier of France argues all night before the National Assembly, and then goes to the bar "for a quick one" to settle his nerves. The movies and television shows delight in picturing the nervous young man who is about to "pop the question" — of course he must first go to a saloon where he orders a "double" to bolster his courage! Yet I do not remember many people who are able to stop after this one short swig or one quick snort. As Goethe says in a line translated by Carlyle: "Choose well; your choice is brief and yet endless."

In the flaming Twenties, the "choice" was again and again made in favor of drink. Genius would flare and then flame away, much as alcohol flares and then burns itself away in moments.

I remember when my brother-in-law happened to mention to me that he had met a bright young novelist, newly clutched to the bosom of the "fashionable set." I asked: "What sort of person is he?" And the answer was: "He and his wife are both drinking themselves to death."

We were talking about F. Scott Fitzgerald, shining star of the jazz-age kaleidoscope of bootleggers, bathtub gin and flappers. Scott and Zelda, his wife, wanted pleasure, and they wanted it fast. They lived fast and they died young — Zelda in a mental institution, Scott in the torments of dipsomania. His friends called him "F. Scotch Fitzgerald." Drink was the central theme of his life — and cynical, confused and tragic drinking was a central theme in his books, which float along on rivers of alcohol. He was a great artist who was converted by liquor into a pathological study.

And his candle did not last the night.

9

In Baltimore, the city where I was born and where many of my relatives made their homes, intellectual thought was dominated by Henry Louis Mencken, whose violent and vitriolic articles against Prohibition, Puritanism, and middle-class morality appeared regularly in the Baltimore *Sun*. Mencken's influence in the 1920's was vast; authorities quoted him, college students adulated and admired him, and his pronouncements made frontpage news. I doubt that anyone was neutral about Mencken; either they were the targets of his barbed attacks, or they exalted him as an inspired enemy of hypocrisy, bigotry and stupidity.

My Uncle Bland — who had generously loaned me two hundred dollars when I could not find a publisher for my first novel — lived in Baltimore. He had been devouring Mencken's essays in the "Sunpaper" for years, but the two had never met. I brought them together for dinner one evening when I was in the city gathering material for a book; and a few words about that event might serve as an introduction to this part of my narrative.

Uncle Bland was one of the richest men in Baltimore. A descendant of John Randolph, the Virginia statesman who for a time served as Speaker of the House, Uncle Bland had moved to Maryland after the Civil War; he had brought with him nothing but determination, an honored name, and business acumen. I remember walking through the downtown business-section with him once, when I was five or six years old. He stopped at the city's leading grocery store, and persuaded the proprietor to buy stock in a projected bonding concern to be called the United States Fidelity and Guarantee Company. The company, with John Randolph Bland as its president, prospered mightily; before long it had branches in every important city in the world.

Once Uncle Bland made a tour of the country to meet his many company agents and executives. He held a banquet in Pasadena for some two hundred employees, filling the largest private dining-room of the biggest local hotel. I was in California at the time, and was invited to attend. We all sang "Annie Laurie" and "Nellie Gray," and a number of other songs calculated to work up family feelings and battle-spirit; and were then exhorted to go out and do our best for U. S. Fidelity and Guarantee, presumably by taking business away from other fellows.

A practical man, Uncle Bland recognized the oncoming of Prohibition before the legislation actually became part of our Constitution in 1918. He laid in a goodly stock of wines, whiskeys, brandies and liqueurs in the cellar of his Catonsville mansion — only the best brands and vintages for John Randolph Bland, and they cost him six thousand dollars in all. Then, as he always did, he moved to his town house for the winter. Thieves entered the mansion by the cellar door, and carried off every case of his treasures.

This loss was the main subject of a dinner party at which I introduced Uncle Bland to Henry Mencken. Mencken told about the brands which he preferred, and my uncle told about the brands which he had stocked. Mencken spoke lovingly of the beers he had sampled in Germany, and Uncle Bland described the wines he had sampled in France. Mencken said everything he had to say on the subject of prohibition, and it was enough to have filled an issue of the "Sunpaper," with material left over for an issue of *The Smart Set*. And every once in a while Mencken would cast a sly glance in my direction, for he knew that nothing could exasperate me more than an evening of drinking and talking about drinking.

In a sense, our relationship for years to come was kept by Mencken on this extraordinarily petty level: his desire to have me recognize whiskey and beer as wholesome and beneficial — or, at the very least, as harmless. Once when he was coming to visit me in California, newspaper reporters interviewed me and asked if I was going to make a Socialist out of Mencken. My answer was yes, that I would if I could. When this comment was reported to Mencken, he replied: "No, I'm going to make a drunkard out of Sinclair." I remember another one of his taunts. Mencken had written a book which I considered an ill-informed and bigoted attack on democracy; he sent it to me with the inscription, "To Upton Sinclair — to make him yell."

My yells were loud, but not nearly so widely-heard as my friend's. In 1924, Henry started a new magazine with George Jean Nathan — the *American Mercury*, a biting, iconoclastic, and wonderfully literate publication which featured contributions by many of America's best-known writers. I "yelled," to use his words, about many of the magazine's policies, particularly the declaration that "this magazine is committed to the return of the American saloon." Mencken answered with the statement that "the question did not permit of discussion."

Too many other things "did not permit of discussion" in his publication. Mencken talked about freedom; all his theories were based on freedom; his praise was for freedom, and his political and economic faith required it. But when he became editor of the *American Mercury*, he practiced strict and rigid control of what writers had to say. He was the final arbiter of what appeared between the arsenic-green covers of *American Mercury*. Sometimes he did not allow the truth to reach print if it controverted his "policies."

I once wrote an article for him about Edward Mac-Dowell, the composer, whose Columbia University music class I had attended. It was a non-controversial piece of reminiscence, and Mencken called it a "charming thing." He wanted me to do other articles, similar ones, about other interesting people I had known. And the first of the series was to be about George Sterling.

But — and this was a big "but" — Mencken stipulated that the article could not mention George's alcoholism. This was impossible; I argued against it, aghast at Mencken's self-delusion that drinking does no harm and has no effects on the writer's mind. But he would not change his position. Not even after the macabre tragedy in which he himself played an unwitting role.

Mencken was in California on a trip. His journey West had occasioned excitement and interest and frivolity. I remember his own diverting account of what happened to him as he crossed the country on the Southern Pacific. The general passenger agent had telegraphed the district superintendent of the railroad line; and this worthy had notified the conductor of the train and all the station agents on the way: *"Mencken is on the train!"* Hospitality did not cease at any hour of the day or night. The Pullman porter conjured up a magical mint julep; the train conductor produced real Scotch, or so at least he said. And at every stop there was a local deputation with flowers and brass bands and beautiful smiling maidens, and admirers congregating to sing "Hail to the Chief!" Mencken was short and solidly made, with bright china-blue eyes and the round rosy face of a cherub. But the rosy face grew apoplectic as he described his weary efforts to close his eyes in sleep while visitors rapped on his compartment door, and bands blared at station stops.

No one could have looked forward with more excitement to Mencken's stay in California than George Sterling. Mencken was more than an editor to George — he was his hero. In a letter George wrote shortly before Mencken's visit, he said: "I just sold an article to Mencken, about a prizefighter I used to tag around after, as a youth of 18. Mencken is to be in Texas in October, and says he is coming on to the coast to visit me for a week, which will stop all this water-wagon nonsense."

George *did* stop the "nonsense." He went off on one of his "tears." Then a reaction of misery and depression set in. And then in the Bohemian Club—the club for which he had written his best work, a play called *Truth* — in this club where he was loved and honored, George swallowed a dose of cyanide of potassium.

Mencken wrote me a letter about Sterling's suicide. "Whatever George told you in moments of katzenjammer," he wrote, "I am sure he got a great deal more fun out of alcohol than woe. It was his friend for many years and made life tolerable. He committed suicide in the end not because he wanted to get rid of drink, but simply because he could no longer drink enough to give him any pleasure."

I published my comment on this statement:

> Was any more poisonous nonsense ever penned by an intellectual man? How many pleasures there are which do not pall with age, and do not destroy their devotees! The pleasure of knowledge, for example — the gaining of it and helping to spread it. The pleasure of sports; I play tennis, and it is just as much fun to me at forty-eight as it was at fourteen. The pleasure of music; I play the violin, after a fashion, and my friend Mencken plays it better, I hope — and does he find that every year he has to play more violently in order to hear it, and that after playing he suffers agonies of sickness, remorse and dread? I say, for shame upon an intellectual man who cannot make such distinctions; for shame upon a teacher of youth who has no care whether he sets their feet upon the road to wisdom and happiness, or to misery and suicide!

Both Henry Mencken and I lived to see time deal with many of the things about which we quarrelled violently in private and in print. We crossed swords during the early years of the *American Mercury,* and I recall making a half-serious offer to write an article analyzing the editor of that magazine, showing how his ignorance of economics made his thinking about the modern world futile. (My suggestion met with no favor!) Again we disagreed violently about alcoholism, and what it did to my beloved friend. And during my campaign for Governor of California, we had vast differences of opinion, and Mencken's editorials about my campaign were persistently incorrect. Our friendship was a long series of feuds, punctuated by cheerful visits and vigorous correspondence until his death early in 1956.

I cannot help but wonder just what other contributions that brilliant, restless mind would have been had it not been so occupied for so many years with the trivia of brands, vintages, and lagers. And I cannot help but wish that he had used his tremendous personality and immense wit not to condone maudlin, drunken sprees — but to prevent them.

On the other hand, Mencken insisted that I have been too much occupied during my life with the *dangers* of drinking. No one would be rash enough, of course, to claim that this "preoccupation" has interfered with the quantity of books and pamphlets and articles that I have produced — for indeed, words have tumbled from my pen with the rapidity of leaves falling from a tree in a gale. As long ago as 1938 — before my "Lanny Budd" books were published — a statistician estimated that some 732 books bearing my name had been published in forty-seven languages in over thirty different countries.

No, their criticism might be that never having been a "social" drinker or a "moderate" drinker, I cannot understand the pleasures of the grape, nor appreciate the warmth it is supposed to generate, nor realize how harmless its effects may be when it is taken with restraint. My answer is that I have had so many other kinds of intoxication — looking at nature, reading great poetry, listening to music, and above all, seeking and getting knowledge, that I have never had the slightest interest in liquor. As a youth, I took on occasional Sundays a sip of Communion wine; it was claret, I believe, but I don't remember the taste. In any event, my thoughts when the wine touched my lips were religious, not those of the gourmet.

Later, when my first books had been published, I was invited by the journalist Arthur Brisbane to meet the Danish critic, George Brandes, who had read and praised my work. We dined in Delmonico's, then New York City's most fashionable restaurant. Brisbane ordered a bottle of champagne; and when I mentioned that I had never tasted it, I was invited to seize the opportunity. I took one sip and said that I could scarcely tell it from apple juice; then I left the rest in the glass while I talked with Brandes about literature and life.

Finally, on a long canoe trip in Canada, we were caught in a cold, penetrating rainstorm, and were soaked to the skin. We had paddled forty miles through a chain of lakes and streams in one day; and when we finally put up a tent and crawled in, I was shivering and blue. I was offered some whiskey and drank a small quantity of it from a tin cup. I immediately felt a warm glow and fell sound asleep, awakening without ill effects from the exhaustion, the cold rain, or the whiskey. I considered this a medicinal use of alcohol, and would use it again under similar circumstances. But none such have arisen in my life.

Obviously, then, I cannot testify on the pleasures of drink. I can remember how often, however, I have seen people who were blind to the pleasures of this astonishing, fascinating world simply because they *did* drink.

Soon after my first books were published, I met Alfred Henry Lewis, a journalist and writer of fiction. Lewis had created an imaginary Arizona town, Wolfville, and he peopled it with an amusing set of characters. He told their stories in such works as *Wolfville Days* and *Wolfville Folks*.

Very much a man about town, Lewis offered to show me the "real New York." We sat in an old hotel on Broadway, and he told me the "inside story" of New York politics, graft and corruption. Then we began to move from popular spot to popular spot, and he introduced me as we went to one Broadway character after another. Before long we were behind the scenes in a theatre, talking to George M. Cohan. He was dressed in his stage costume—gay summer clothes, a straw hat, a fancy little bamboo cane. Then came the signal for him to go on stage, and we heard the opening chorus of "Give My Regards to Broadway." And we moved out again into the Broadway night, off to the famed drinking place named "Considine's." Here I was introduced to a genial confidence man; then to two other men, described as "the best burglar in New York" and "the finest forger in all the United States." Next I met a Supreme Court judge, and a Tammany Hall politician who had been so bold in his depredations that he had been put under indictment. Then out into Broadway we went again, for a tour of the "night spots."

They were neither so elaborate nor expensive in those days, and the entertainment consisted only of a piano and some nasal singing. But I remember in each place the sight of men and women half-asleep and heavy-lidded, alone in secret communion with their liquor-filled glasses. This had been the sight I had seen all through the night—people, sodden and dazed, out for "a good time." And I thought how many wonderful things there are in this world, so much to do and so much to learn—and so much of it being lost in exchange for the measly, momentary "warm glow" of whiskey.

All my life I have been able to say that I am "drunk without alcohol." To me this universe is one vast mystery story, fascinating beyond any power of words to tell. If I could have my own way, I would stay here a million years to watch what happens.

I am anxious to know "what is going to happen next." I want to know more about what really happened in the past, and I read history. I am also absorbed by astronomy, and by the amazing discoveries which men are making with the new tools of this science: reflecting telescopes, radio telescopes, spectroscopes. I belong to the Astronomical Society of the Pacific, and I read their bulletins, and it is as if I see the incredible universe expanding before my eyes. The nearest of the fixed stars is some twenty trillion miles away; and now the 200-inch telescope on Mount Palomar is exploring galaxies which are a billion light-years away, each galaxy having billions of stars like our own galaxy.

Recently I read an article by Harlow Shapley in which he discusses the chances of there being other worlds inhabited by intelligent life. Figuring the probabilities on a mathematical basis, he says there should exist a hundred million inhabited planets, large and small. How I would like to visit them— and some day I may, since both Kant and Einstein have told us that space and time are forms of our thinking.

And then there is the infinitely small universe which science has discovered in the nucleus of the atom. Apparently there are as many nuclear particles in a drop of water as there are stars in the heavens; and who can guess what may turn up inside a proton? We already have found within the atom the power to destroy a city; any day now we may develop the power to heal the world.

And all my life, I have been "drunk" with the intoxicating wonders of good books. With the right book, the world is yours; it waits by your bedside, at your convenience. You can watch the whole pageant of history. You can enter into and share the experiences of the greatest minds that have ever lived on earth. You can, in the words of Tennyson, "dip into the future, far as human eye can see." You can climb to the top of Mount Everest; now for the first time you can go down a mile into the bottom of the sea; you can visit climes hot and cold without discomfort; you can go among strange people and marvel at their ways of survival; you can hunt wild beasts or catch great fish; you can fly to the farthest galaxies and penetrate the infinite minuteness of the atomic nucleus; you can go inside your own body; you can go to Heaven with the saints and to Hell with Dante.

In a world like this, one does not commit suicide "simply because he could no longer drink enough to give him any pleasure!"

10

EARLY IN 1928 I completed *Boston,* a novel which had the Sacco-Venzetti case as its major theme. The publishers were going to great expense and labor for it; and one custom of the time was to give a grand party and invite the critics to come and meet the author.

Craig and I made the trip to New York. "Can't you make him get a new suit for the occasion?" begged the publishers. And so Craig invited me for a walk (most unusual in and of itself!) and lured me into a store. She persuaded me to buy a black suit, since this is what her father, Judge Kimbrough, had always worn. Very dignified it was—and twenty-eight years later I still have it in the closet, in case I should ever wish to be dignified again.

The party was held in the ballroom of the Savoy-Plaza Hotel. Tables against one wall, covered with all sorts of delicacies; fifty or sixty literary lights; all the guests gracious and smiling; music, and even some dancing. I led the grand march with Mrs. George Sylvester Vierick—she in a cloth-of-gold costume, I in my dignified black suit.

All the critics complimented me on *Boston,* and went away and forgot it in a few weeks. A new book in New York is like water poured on a hot stove; it makes a loud noise, but is soon gone.

While we were in New York, however, we took two new friends into our lives, Bill and Helen Woodward. William E. Woodward is best remembered as the author of two splendid biographies, one of George Washington and the other of General Grant. When we met him, his bestseller was *Bunk,* a book I greatly admired. A dinner party was planned at their home.

Craig and I went to the apartment hotel where the Woodwards lived, and travelled through a hallway to a door which stood open. A large Southern gentleman of the old school was standing there, erect and smiling. When we came up to him, he opened his arms wide and took us both into an embrace of hospitality. We, who are of medium size, were dwarfed by his stature; and Helen, the tiny woman who was his wife, seemed to be a fragile figurine at his side. Helen's smile was bright and sweet, and we felt immediately that we had escaped from a tornado in the streets to a haven of peace and warmth.

Bill Woodward's career in letters was a unique one. Until the age of fifty, he was an important figure in the financial world—senior vice-president of the Industrial Finance Corporation of New York, parent organization of the Morris Plan Banks. Helen Richardson Dreiser, who worked as Bill's secretary at one time, tells in *My Life with Dreiser* how Mr. Woodward paused, one day, while dictating a letter or memorandum to her. He gazed out of the window and said:

"When I am fifty, I shall chuck this financial game completely . . . I shall *write* . . . when I am fifty."

Surrounded always by fine books and stimulating people, Bill Woodward became a beloved figure in the literary world. His friendships were legion; and at his home we met a fascinating author-traveller, William Seabrook.

I had heard of him long ago, back in Greenwich Village; he had gone to live among the desert Arabs for a year or two, and had written a book about it. Then he lived among the natives in Haiti, and learned about voodoo. Then among cannibals in Africa. And out of each experience had come a book. He was delightful company, and offered to journey out to California and live near us—perhaps so that he could write still another book of "amazing experiences!"

But I cannot be light-hearted about the place where Seabrook did go some years later. He went to Bloomingdale, an insane asylum up the Hudson River. And he tells about it in an extraordinary book called *Asylum*.

"I had asked for it," he writes in the preface. "I mean, I had asked for it literally, though I hadn't specified any particular sort of place. I had been begging, pleading, demanding toward the last, to be locked up . . . shut up . . . chained up . . . anything . . . and had begun to curse and blame my dearest friends for what seemed to me their failure to realize how desperately, how stupidily, I needed to be shut up where I couldn't get out and where I couldn't get my hands on a bottle. I had become a confirmed, habitual drunkard, without any of the stock alibis, or excuses."

He was well treated in this place, and after seven months he came out, to all appearances completely cured. But as you read his book, you wonder if he is going to *stay* cured. He writes: "God forbid that any of this record be or become a temperance lecture. I still think whiskey is a grand thing.

I still believe that no man has ever become a victim of whiskey —but only of some weakness within himself."

We find him rationalizing, just as Jack London did in *John Barleycorn*. Bill Seabrook tells us that it is all right to drink because you want to, and that the danger only begins when you drink because you have to.

Then you read the unhappy sequel in his autobiography, *No Hiding Place*, published seven years after *Asylum*. Near the end of the book you find these sentences: "I was miserable, made Marjorie (his wife) miserable, and before I knew it, I was drinking again in the mornings when I didn't want to drink, not for the pleasure but in the desperate false hope that I might write a page or two that wasn't wooden, and presently because I no longer dared to face the typewriter. Sometimes I'd go to bed sodden at dark, awaken before Marjorie in the still pitch-black darkness before dawn, stumble up to the barn without breakfast, and be sodden again by sunrise." And on the next page we find him shouting at himself in the mirror: "He's a drunkard. What do drunkards do? *They* ... *drink* ... *themselves* ... *to* ... *death!*"

And so William Seabrook came to realize that it is *not* "all right to drink because you want to." Yet this is apparently an immensely difficult concept for intelligent, moderate, occasional drinkers to appreciate; and their annoyance at warnings and preachments of the sort I have sometimes been wont to give is enormous. I "spoil their fun."

When Bill and Helen Woodward came to visit us in Pasadena, for example, we took them to dine at one of the old hotels which were becoming mementos of the grandeur that had existed in this winter home of millionaires. I ordered grape juice. Bill studied the menu and ordered apple juice. Then his voice rose querulously as he said: "All of this misery because of Upton! It might have been champagne!" He jumped up from the table and strode from the dining room. A few minutes later he returned. "I'll tell you what's the matter with *you*, Upton," he said, sternly. "You live in this God-forsaken town where there's nothing but churches on the street corners." He grumbled still more about our town throughout dinner; and when we were saying goodnight, he announced, "I won't be seeing *you* tomorrow, Upton. Dreiser lives in Hollywood and I'm going to see *him*."

Thus, at times, I have nettled the feelings of friends. It has always been a difficult choice to make: Is one going to lose friendships because he inveighs against drink? Or must he run the risk of losing his friends *to* drink!

My answer has been to speak frankly at all times. It is a habit of many years . . . it is yet another crusade.

At the end of 1929 there was a dreadful collapse in the stock market. The average man, who did not gamble in stocks, paid little attention to it; but it turned out that all industry was dependent upon speculation, and the depression spread from Wall Street to the entire country. Thousands of factories shut down, banks failed, farmers lost their farms on mortgages, and unemployment spread like a plague. There were among them many from the highly-educated classes—lawyers, doctors, engineers, writers, and so on. Six hundred lawyers were dropped from the Los Angeles Bar Association because they could not pay their annual dues of seven dollars and a half. The newspapers kept telling us that business would soon pick up, but it didn't; the months stretched into years—four years—and in California, with a population of seven million, one in seven was without work; many were starving.

A chairman of the County Central Committee of the Democratic Party came to me with a proposition: "Enroll as a Democrat and announce yourself as a candidate for the nomination for Governor. The people know your books and trust you; tell them exactly what you will do to deal with this depression, and you will sweep the state."

To run for office was the last thing in the world I wanted. But I recalled that my great-grandfather, Commodore Arthur Sinclair, had been one of the founders of the Democratic Party. It was my birthright; maybe I should claim it!

I got to thinking about the problem; what would I do? A life-long "co-opper," I became fascinated by the idea. I had been reading and thinking about "production for use" for three decades. I worked out in my mind a complete schedule: a state-supported body to purchase or rent land and establish production of food for the use of the producers, the hungry unemployed and their families; the same for factory production, and the same for the financing of both.

At that time Los Angeles County alone had 509,000 persons being supported on relief. At fifty cents per person per day, that was a hundred million dollars a year—and all of it pure loss to the taxpayers. On the other hand, the self-help co-operatives were keeping 150,000 members alive with aid from the state of only seventeen cents per member per month. The economy of that required no argument. But it was opposed by the "conservatives" for the same reason that TVA is being opposed today; it was what many people consider "Creeping Socialism."

The rest of my program included: a graduated income tax, old age pensions, and a tax on idle land held for speculation. I sat myself down and wrote a pamphlet entitled: I, *Governor of California: And How I Ended Poverty*. The slogan was to be "End Poverty in California," which spelled EPIC. I went into full detail; I told exactly how I "did" it, and it was so convincing that I almost felt I *had* already done it!

When I showed the manuscript to those who wanted to turn me into a politician, it was like throwing gasoline into a fire. They laid siege to me, and would not take "No" for my answer. My dear wife was horrified; here was another Crusade. She had just got back a little of her health—and now she was going to lose it all again! I hesitated on the brink, while the pamphlet was put into type. I registered as a Democrat, thinking I could do it quietly; but this was foolish, of course. The newspapers got hold of it. Then I wanted to back out; it would have been funny if it hadn't been so tragic—my wife wouldn't *let* me back out! It was a matter of honor. She would die before she would let me change my mind after I had once committed myself.

Well, we were in for it; and it was like being caught up in a whirlwind and swept out over a vast uncharted sea. My elderly secretary lived in a small cottage, and I rented the living room from her; people poured into it, and it became the first EPIC headquarters. Presently EPIC rented the whole cottage, and then it moved to a larger one, until at the end it had a building with thirty-two rooms. I printed 20,000 copies of my pamphlet, and they were gone in a couple of weeks; I printed some more, and then turned the plates over to headquarters. The campaign was financed by the sale of that and three other EPIC pamphlets I wrote—435,000 books at a quarter a copy; also from the collections taken up at my mass meetings all over the state. We had no money at the start, and we never received a dollar from the Democratic Party funds. Under state law, school auditoriums may be used free for political meetings at night, and we made use of that privilege. For almost a year I went up and down the state, and the meetings grew bigger and bigger.

The primary campaign lasted ten months—that is, so far as EPIC was concerned. Seven other Democratic candidates entered the list; the leading one, favored by the regular Democratic machine, was the political journalist George Creel. When I spoke in the Civic Auditorium in Oakland, I was told that he had spoken there the previous night, and had discussed me, saying, "Sinclair has the brains of a pigeon." I repeated this to the great throng, and replied: "I don't know much about the anatomy of pigeons, and I doubt if Creel does either; but this I do know, that nobody ever saw ten million pigeons starving to death when the ground was covered with corn and the trees were full of cherries."

The primary election was held on August 28, and my vote was 436,000; Creel's was 228,000, and the rest trailed; my vote was a majority over all the other seven put together. I was the Democratic Party's candidate for Governor, and the legally chosen head of the party. It was the biggest vote ever cast in a California primary election.

It was a furious campaign; people took sides, and families were split up. A lady of one of the oldest families of California wrote to my wife that in one drawing room she had seen enraged people throwing sofa pillows at one another—which, I suppose, is at least more elegant than throwing brickbats. A business man of Beverly Hills told me about the experience of his daughter, a high-school girl. She had been invited to the home of a schoolmate, and there, at the dinner table, the head of the house denounced Upton Sinclair. The guest remarked, "I heard him speak, and I thought what he said was sensible." The answer was, "Nobody can talk like that in my house. Get up and get out!" And he meant it; he drove her out!

EPIC was completely a ground-roots movement, sudden and spontaneous. It had no help from the regular Democratic machine, or from any other machine or "big interest." It was amateurish and chaotic, learning from its own mistakes when it learned at all. I would be grabbed up at short notice, or with none at all, and driven away to a mass meeting about which nobody had remembered to notify me. I called myself a "speech-making machine," one that was bundled into a car, then carried onto a platform—where somebody pressed a button to make it talk. I would be driven by a couple of college boys in my own worn-out car. Or a wealthy playboy would take me in his imported sports car, enjoying the excitement without really knowing why. Craig has never forgotten how, at a meeting in San Diego, I was so exhausted that I wavered, and two men came and held me up while I spoke. And then they carried me out on burly shoulders to address an overflow meeting in the park adjoining the auditorium.

"You boys are killing him!" she pleaded once; and the answer of one was, "Well, he has to die sometime." She came back at this young man by declaring: "I'll see that when he does, he doesn't die for *you!*" From then on she set herself and others to watch him, and it wasn't long before she knew where his attitude had come from—Moscow. That is an aspect of the campaign which must not be left out of the story. At the outset, the Communists poured ridicule upon EPIC; they would print leaflets denouncing it, and scatter them from the gallery over the heads of the audience; when that happened, I would call for one of the leaflets and read it from the platform and answer it. They called EPIC "one more rotten egg from the Blue Buzzard's nest." (It was the period of the New Deal's effort to find work for the unemployed, and there was a symbol known as "the Blue Eagle.") But when the Communists saw that EPIC was becoming a "band-wagon", they quit ridiculing it and took to infiltrating; they would come to work in the headquarters, and in all the clubs —and they would even start clubs of their own!

I was not elected. I got 879,000 votes, but my Republican opponent received a little over a million.

On Election Night we had several close friends with us, listening to the returns over the radio. Everyone was tense; and when it became evident that I was running behind, our friends were decorously silent. Then, over the radio, some political authority declared that the outcome was certain; "Sinclair has lost." Craig's knees gave way suddenly and she sank to the floor, weeping and laughing at the same time, and crying: "Oh, thank God! thank God! thank God!" Lewis Browne, who was one of our dear friends in California, came to her and said: "We understand, Craig. We all hoped he would lose." She had worked hard for victory as a matter of duty. But in her heart she did not want me to win. They all believed victory would mean death by overwork or assassination.

Indeed, shortly after the campaign I learned from unassailable sources that a Beverly Hills businessman had made up his mind to see to it personally that I never governed California. He arranged all his affairs, made his will, and told his family what he was going to do. He was going to be present at the radio station where I was scheduled to speak if I won the election; and there he was going to shoot me!

My own point of view on Election Night was this: I could say with satisfaction that I had helped to educate the people of California, as well as many across the nation, to the power of the ballot. I had also taught them the need for taking an active part in politics, if they wanted to win next time. The magazine *Unity* commented at the time:

"What Sinclair did in one year was to shake the state with an earthquake mightier than that which toppled the towers of San Francisco a generation ago . . . The methods used in defeating Sinclair were perhaps unprecedented in terms of sheer wickedness and villainy. Every crime but murder was shamelessly resorted to. The legions of hell were let loose on this man."

Regrettably, I was defeated by those whom we like to consider the leaders of the "good people" in the American community—prominent businessmen, editors and columnists of major newspapers, the well-to-do and respectable and conservative.

Yet the despair of the Depression could not be wiped away by promises and campaigns; and so during those long years of economic chaos, thousands of Americans turned to new ideologies in their quest for security.

Some became Communists. In a lifetime of political and economic activity, I have come to know Communists and Communism. I have experienced the insidiousness of their methods; I have lost friends to their fold; and I have seen how they use liquor in their unceasing war against freedom.

11

I LEARNED TO my distress recently that the Reds are using novels I wrote thirty, forty and fifty years ago in their present propaganda campaigns in Europe and Asia. They quote my indictments of an earlier time's inequities, and pass the material off labeled "a picture of life in the United States today." Thus it is that I write as often as possible for foreign publications, or send my messages abroad on the Voice of America.

Not long ago I was asked to address a message to three million readers of *Yomiuri Shimbun,* a Japanese periodical. The editors asked me to predict the possibilities of world peace; and in one paragraph of my answer, I sketched the history of dismay and disillusion with which American liberals have watched the growth of world Communism:

> The problem which confronts us all is that of
> an organized system of terrorism and dictatorship

which calls itself 'democratic,' and uses the phrases of self-government to fool the oppressed peoples of the earth . . .

When the Russian Tsardom was overthrown thirty-eight years ago, I rejoiced, as did all liberal-minded persons. When the Bolsheviks overthrew the Socialist government and made a deal with the generals of the German Kaiser, I was saddened. But I hoped for the best . . .

I did not know then that Lenin had set down in his writings that it would be necessary for the Bolsheviks to lie and deceive in order to get their way. He wrote that, and he did that, and his successors are doing it on a world-wide scale today. . . .

Those fanatical men of violence, the Communists, want to put all true democrats into slave-labor camps, and make the rest of the people into slave laborers at home. They have done that in eleven countries of Europe now behind the Iron Curtain, and with their Red Chinese allies they have an elaborate and cold-blooded program to do it over the rest of the world.

So that I can show you how world Communism used talented American writers in its never-ending war against democracy, I will briefly tell you the story of a motion-picture film titled *Thunder Over Mexico.*

Sergei Eisenstein was Soviet Russia's leading motion-picture director. His relations with the regime became strained, and in 1930 he journeyed to Hollywood—only to be coolly received by America's film industry as well. In order to cover up his failure he conceived the idea of going into Mexico and making a travelog of the primitive Indians.

He sent someone to ask me to assist in raising twenty-five thousand dollars for that purpose; and I, thinking to help a great artist—which he was—persuaded some friends to put up the money. Eisenstein signed a contract to make a strictly non-political picture for this sum, and to finish it in three or four months. He went and stayed a year, extracting more money from us by the threat that if we didn't send it there would be no picture. Later on we found out why he had been stalling; he was trying to get a contract to make his next picture in the Argentine, in Japan, in India—any place in the world, in fact, in order to keep from having to go back to the Soviet Union.

In the end we learned that no promise he made had any meaning, and so we cut off the funds. We tried to work out an arrangement with the Soviet Government, but they, too, broke every promise they made, and we soon realized that their word meant nothing. So we arranged to have the picture cut in Hollywood; and instantly all the fury of Communist propaganda was turned against us. Not merely in the United States, but all over the world, grotesque falsehoods about the project were spread in newspapers and periodicals and books.

A veritable siege was laid upon us. There came authors, journalists, artists, actors, every kind of person who could find any excuse for taking an interest in the film. Some of them were Communist agents; other were fellow-travelers; and still others were dupes, men and women truly interested in cinematic art. They all wanted to see the uncut film; they all praised it extravagantly; and then they had all said the same thing—that it would be a "crime against art" to have that picture cut by anyone but "the great master who had conceived and created it." The fact that he had taken the money of both friends and strangers, the fact that my wife and I had mortgaged our home and had gone head-over-heels into debt to save the picture—all this meant nothing. We must "give it to the Soviet Union," knowing full well that we would never see a foot of it again. End of the story: the picture cost ninety thousand dollars and earned about thirty thousand.

Among those who came to plead, cajole or threaten were two of America's immortal writers—Sherwood Anderson and Theodore Dreiser.

In the middle twenties I had read a new novel by an unknown writer. It was called *Windy McPherson's Son,* and it gave me a particular thrill because it showed real knowledge of poverty, and true tenderness for the poor. In those days our successful writers seldom condescended to be aware of poverty. So I wrote a letter to Sherwood Anderson, congratulating him—and, as usual, trying to bring him to my social point of view. He answered on the letterhead of an advertising firm in Chicago, and we developed a correspondence. He said:

"To me there is no answer for the terrible confusion of life. I want to try and sympathize and to understand a little of the twisted and maimed life that industrialism has brought on us. But I can't solve things, Sinclair. I can't do it. Man, I don't know who is right and who wrong." And he added, "Damn it, you have made me go on like a propagandist, you should be ashamed of yourself."

There came a second novel, *Marching Men,* the story of a labor leader who rouses the workers—and for what? To march! Where shall they march? He doesn't know. What shall they march for? He doesn't know that. What does their marching symbolize? Nobody knows; but march and keep on marching—"Out of Nowhere into Nothing," to quote the title of a Sherwood Anderson short story.

Even in childhood, Anderson wanted to create beauty—
yet so severe was his poverty that once his only food was a
mound of cabbages which rowdies had thrown at his mother's
door at night. Then he had to go out into the world of
hustle and graft to fight for a living; he became manager
of a paint factory, without the least interest in any kind of
paint. And all the while the suppressed artist in him sobbed
and suffered, lived its own subconscious life, and occasionally
surged up to the surface—driving the respectable paint-
factory manager to actions which his stenographer and office
force considered insane. It drove him to drop the paint job,
suddenly, abruptly, right in the middle of dictating a letter;
it drove him to a nervous breakdown, and the life of a wanderer; it drove him to throw up the advertising job in Chicago which he had when he first wrote to me. Finally, it
helped make him a man of genius.

Sherwood Anderson was forty before his first novel was
published. Once critical success came, however, he wrote
book after book. And each of them, I found, had his own
thwarted personality as its central theme. In *Windy Mc-
Pherson's Son* he tells the artist's story; and then he tells it
again, with some variations, in *Poor White*. His painful frus-
trations are depicted in *A Story Teller's Story;* his childhood
is pictured in *Tar*. His own experiences with marriage are
the drive behind *Many Marriages* and *Dark Laughter*. His
frustrated personality and philosophy are bared in *Notebook*
—and even his short stories present one or another aspect of
a man in conflict with himself.

I was astonished when Sherwood Anderson came to
argue with me about the Eisenstein film. He was not a Party
member; his political theories were ephemeral. (At one point,
he edited two newspapers in Marion, Virginia—one was Democratic, the other Republican!) But we ran the uncut ver-

sion of the film for him, and like everybody else, he was enraptured by its beautiful scenes. "Don't cut it," he said. "Send it to Russia—they'll have Eisenstein cut it." We told him of our grim experiences with the director. "What has that got to do with his being a great artist?" Anderson asked. "A great artist is above morality."

The argument continued over lunch some days later. My memory is that he had brought a flask along, and sampled some on the drive; by the time we were all assembled at the luncheon table, Sherwood was "high."

His work deteriorated in his later years. In *A Story Teller's Story*, he speaks of a "fluency in words that never comes to me when I am writing, and it only comes to my lips when I am slightly under the influence of strong drink." Presently we find him talking about "morning coffee, containing a touch of brandy." Just a touch!

Anderson died at sea, on a liner bound for Brazil. Abdominal congestion and peritonitis were brought on when he swallowed the toothpick in a cocktail-sausage at the "farewell party" given him in the ship's stateroom. Ben Hecht, who drank wine with Anderson in New York's fashionable Twenty-One the night before Anderson's departure, wrote a newspaper column about their reunion. It was grimly prophetic: Anderson, he said, seemed like a man leaving not a country but life, like a wearied animal going off to an unfamiliar place to die.

Another writer who intervened in the matter of the motion picture was Theodore Dreiser. I had met him as early as 1908, when he was editor-in-chief of the Butterick publications, fashion magazines. His novel, *Sister Carrie*, had been published and suppressed, and I had never seen it. Then *Jennie Gerhardt* was published, and I knew we had a great writer.

Dreiser's life had been a hard one: he had come up from the bottom, beginning in Chicago about the time of the World's Fair, 1893. Edgar Lee Masters and Sherwood Anderson were there at the same time, all three grubbing for an existence in a hateful environment. Dreiser wandered the streets, a homeless, jobless, miserable youth. In *A Book About Myself* he tells of reading newspaper columns by Eugene Field, and he remarks: "This comment on local life here and now, these transient bits on local street scenes, institutions, characters, functions, all moved me as nothing hitherto had." He was storing thousands of such details in his mind, preparing to weave them into huge patterns.

He wanted to be a newspaper man, but didn't know how to begin; he hung around a newspaper office like a poor stray dog, until people got tired of kicking him out and finally gave him something to write. Then he tells us, "Men, as I was beginning to find—all of us—were small, irritable, nasty in their struggle for existence." Such was the world in which a "realist" formed his mind.

I remember him as a big silent fellow, a good listener. I could not imagine why he wanted to be editor of such uninteresting magazines; but later on, when I read *The "Genius"*, I saw that he had been watching the literary and artistic world of New York, and had been shaping it in his mind. Then when I read *An American Tragedy* I knew he had put into it all his understanding of the hapless people he had known in boyhood and youth. He was a graceless and awkward writer, but he had a soul full of pity for the miseries he had seen around him, and that made him one of the great spirits of our time. I loved him for it, and went all-out for *An American Tragedy*. My words were: "Theodore Dreiser has given us one of the world's greatest novels."

When the Eisenstein affair was on the front pages,

Dreiser wrote me a letter of strong protest about my refusal to ship the film off to Moscow. My wife replied with a detailed account of what had happened; and his reply was yes, we had been imposed upon; and yes, we were entirely in the right. But Dreiser was so much a tool of the Communists that I feared they would soon talk him into reversing his stand again.

He was a man with a violent temper. His wife relates how he got into a dispute with his publisher, Horace Liveright, over the division of the $90,000 paid for the film rights of *An American Tragedy*. They were at lunch in a hotel restaurant and Horace called Theodore a liar. Theodore threw a cup of coffee into Liveright's face. On another occasion he slapped Sinclair Lewis publicly when Lewis accused him of having plagiarized material about Soviet Russia written by Dorothy Thompson, the journalist who became Lewis's wife. Both had been in Moscow at the same time, and apparently both had used the same propaganda material issued by the regime.

Helen Dreiser, who became his wife shortly before his death, tells of an episode back in the days before the writing of *The American Tragedy*. He telephoned that he needed her, and she came in haste.

When I arrived at his studio I found him lying on his day-bed apparently unconscious. I was terrified. He lay there as if the outer shell or personality had dropped from him ...

He said he had been at a party at Carl Van Vechten's and had been brought home ... After going around the corner to a drug store to obtain something to sober him, I got him into his pajamas with difficulty as he was completely paralyzed. He then lapsed into a deep sleep ...

The next morning he awakened perfectly normal. He was extremely surprised to see me there, for he did not remember one thing about calling me the night before, which I thought strange. How did he remember the telephone number in such a condition, I asked myself.

In the same book, Mrs. Dresier reports on her husband's work habits in his last months: "In the morning while I was preparing breakfast, he would bathe, shave, and then, immaculately dressed, walk into the kitchen and pour himself a small drink before sitting down to the table."

He was a man who wandered about from one set of ideas to another, not realizing their incongruity. Floyd Dell reports, "When I saw him later he was somehow an anti-Semitic Nazi and a Russified Communist at the same time." In a letter to Mencken, for example, Dreiser complained of Franklin D. Roosevelt's hostility toward Hitler and his sympathy for the allied powers.

"I begin to suspect that Hitler is correct," he wrote. "The president may be partly Jewish. His personal animosity toward Hitler has already resulted in placing America in the Allied Camp—strengthening Britain's attitude and injuring Germany in the eyes of the world. The brass!"

A year later, Dreiser was announcing his support of Earl Browder, Communist Party leader, for the Presidency of the United States. Thus he went from extreme to extreme, from position to position.

Dreiser was no reeling drunkard, no down-and-out rotgut drinker. My feeling is that his perceptions were sometimes blurred by drink, often confusing his noble heart. I recall that he came to visit us one night, enough "under the influence" to fall asleep in his chair while he was talking and when people were talking with him. At his request we had asked a prominent medium, Arthur Ford, to demonstrate some aspects of psychic research. During the demonstration, Dreiser was asked to corroborate several details about an old newspaper friend. He seemed confused, unable to recollect important events of his past life. Helen Dreiser, who had been at our house with him, called the next day; she apologized for his "condition."

Dreiser would have said that he drank socially, with his friends. The sad fact is, however, that the friends who joined him in this "social tippling" as he grew older were often Communists, there to get his support and use his prestige for the Party's selfish ends. A group of sympathizers prepared a manifesto for him, and he signed it. It was published in the *Daily Worker*, and gave heart to Communists everywhere. They swarmed around him; they extracted more quotes from him, adding to the many articles he had prepared at their behest. And then, a few months later, Dreiser died. It was, truly, an American tragedy.

The Communists use liquor as a sort of Geiger-counter, probing for the weaknesses of men and women. They have used it to gain recruits; they have used it to steal a nation's most guarded secrets.

Mary McCarthy, the brilliant writer of short stories, recently told in *Reporter* magazine how in her youth she flitted about on the outskirts of the Communist movement, attending their dances and drinking parties. Everybody became extremely drunk, and "the atmosphere was horribly sordid."

When the Communist regime was launched in Russia, there were some sincere if mistaken idealists among the "old Bolsheviks"—men and women who really believed in freedom, who were actually convinced that they were uplifting humanity. But thinkers of this sort went down, one after another, in one blood purge after another. They were exterminated as if they had been the most dangerous of snakes.

One of the early forms their idealism took was the prohibition of alcoholic liquor. But that hope died with all the others. The brutal men who came out on top in Russia knew that a drunken people would be easier to hold in subjection than a sober people.

Today the Soviet Union has repudiated all the virtues of the old order and adapted only its evils. The production of liquor is a State monopoly; and the men who control that monopoly live in luxury. Ninety percent of the money paid for every quart of liquor goes directly to the State. Correspondents come home from Russia and report that there are no shoes available in the stores, no clothing, only the basic foodstuffs—and liquor. There's always plenty of liquor.

In France, it was the Communists who were most vociferous in their campaign of hate, ridicule and contempt when Pierre Mendès-France began his historic attempt to curb alcoholism in his country. Again they acted in the knowledge that a wine-sodden nation, sick in mind and body, is easy prey.

And look at the drinking "traditions" of France the Communists there so righteously defended! The nation's consumption of wine in 1954 was six billion bottles—five times as much as Italy, the world's second in wine-consumption. Home distilling is legal in France, with 3,250,000 individuals licensed to produce alcohol from grapes, apples, prunes, pears, sugar beets, and even artichokes. There is one drink shop for every ninety inhabitants. In Germany the ratio is one to 246 people; in Norway, it's one to every three thousand. As a result, there are twenty-two alcoholics to each one thousand inhabitants in France. And at least partially as a result of that fact, I believe, France has the sickest government in the free world, including in its Assembly more Communists than any other free nation of the world.

Liquor works for the Communists in New York and Paris and in Moscow. It works overtime—it gave them the H-bomb.

I take this story from *World* magazine for January, 1954:

> On August 12, 1953, Dr. Bruno Pontecorvo, an Italian-born physicist, exploded a thermonuclear device northeast of the town of Yarkand in Soviet-controlled Sinkiang. At least in principle, this feat gave Russia equality in the atomic arms race.

The story then introduces a rising young English diplomat named Donald Maclean. I quote:

> Assigned to the Egyptian capital as Counselor of Embassy, Maclean had attained greater success than most career diplomats of thirty-five even hope for. And yet he detested his job. The corrupt and decadent society of Egypt enraged and depressed him; he began to drink heavily. At odds with himself and the world, he developed a split personality and, under the influence of alcohol, formed homosexual attachments. Melinda considered a divorce but was deterred by the fear of scandal.
>
> Maclean's emotions reached a violent climax at a house-boat party on the Nile. In a drunken outburst, he wrested a rifle from a guard and menaced the twenty guests. A courageous friend subdued him. The Foreign Office immediately recalled him to London, gave him six months' sick

leave and ordered him to take psychiatric treatment. Only his outstanding record saved him from
summary dismissal.

Those six months of enforced leave, from May
to November 1950, were crucial in the life of Donald Maclean. He was approached by Soviet agents
who, after the arrest of Klaus Fuchs, were badly
in need of a replacement. Maclean proved amen-
able. He was told that "Red China" would build
golden bridges for the right atomic scientist. Maclean suggested Pontecorvo. Another Soviet contact
in the Foreign Office and a friend of Maclean,
Guy Burgess, arranged the details. On July 25,
Pontecorvo and his family left England for an
extended vacation on the Continent. On Septem-
ber 2, after flying from Stockholm to Helsinki,
Finland, on the edge of the Iron Curtain, the Pon-
tecorvos disappeared.

In November, on the recommendation of his
psychiatrist, Donald Maclean was "reintegrated"
into the Foreign Service and made head of the
American Division, proof that his loyalty was un-
questioned at that time. In health and manner he
seemed much improved. Melinda bought a house
in Kent with $20,000 she had inherited. Donald,
now a happy family man, was looking forward to
the birth of a third child. The marriage appeared
definitely saved.

Yet slowly the clouds were gathering over his
head. His conscience bothered him; he reverted
to drink. He began to make strange, brooding
remarks about "Communists agents." When Burgess, who in the meantime had been sent to Wash-

ington, was recalled for personal misconduct, Soviet operatives warned both men that their time was running out. On May 25, 1951—Donald's birthday—Burgess received a telephone call at 5:30 p.m. That evening they drove to Southampton and crossed the Channel aboard the ferry Falaise.

Neither one was seen for almost five years. And then in February of 1956, Burgess and Maclean were put on display at a press conference. The meeting was held in the Kremlin.

12

Our home in California has been a waystop for poets and politicians, writers and actors, philosophers and journalists. Here we've been visited by old friends on their way to an assignment in Hollywood or a vacation in the sun. Years later, on occasion, the sons or daughters of these friends have themselves come to bring us news and anecdotes and reports of their family's fortunes. This is one of the rewards of a long life, and one of the advantages of living near a "crossroads of the world."

It is a joy to play host to young people bursting and alive with talent. Yet we remember moments when the pleasure was mixed with pain, when we could see youthful ability and idealism confused and confounded by compulsive drinking.

Such was the story of Klaus Mann, son of the genius universally considered to have been the greatest novelist of our time. Klaus and Erika, his sister, knew many cities and towns of their own continent. Now they were journeying to the United States, on their way to see the rest of the world. I admired and had corresponded with Thomas Mann, their father; now I was going to meet two of his children.

Our conversations in Pasadena were pleasant, and when the young travellers went off they wrote pleasant things about me, which does not always happen. From that time on I exchanged letters with Klaus, sent him some of my books, and received his in return.

In 1942, Klaus published his autobiography *The Turning Point.* In it he was frank, in a quiet and decent way, and his words help us understand those Europeans who grew up with a world falling to pieces about them. He explains the Jazz Age in one explicit sentence: "We could hardly deviate from any ethical norm, for the cogent reason that there was none."

He tells us that he and his sister were known to the neighbors as "those terrible Mann children." Their experiments in living were often wild and dangerous, and the two did not always get along with their distinguished father.

Preparing to visit the United States, Klaus talked with Sinclair Lewis, then in Europe. Hal's advice was, "Have a hell of a time." And Klaus notes concerning Hal that he was "in the habit of emptying whiskey glasses." In Greenwich Village they were shown about by Horace Liveright, and here the two young visitors could observe "a plentitude of attractive girls, and all of them seemed rather fond of gin." They met Henry Louis Mencken, champion of the American saloon, and Henry's contribution to the education of Erika and Klaus was this: "I know hundreds, perhaps thousands of Americans. All of them drink liquor . . . Well, let's open another bottle. *Prost!*"

And then they journeyed out to Hollywood, and there met Emil Jannings, the actor, making a thousand dollars a day; and Greta Garbo, coming in and announcing, "I am so terribly tired. May I have a whiskey?" In California the young visitors were almost killed in a car accident, and Klaus's remark following the experience was, "We had quite a few drinks—champagne, beer, and Scotch. The brakes of the age-old Ford hardly worked."

Then we find them in Paris with Jean Cocteau. What he contributes to their philosophy is this: "Liquor provokes paroxysms of folly; opium produces paroxysms of wisdom."

And next Klaus is in Morocco, experimenting with hashish. He says at this point: "I have lost more friends through suicide (including the less direct patterns of self-destruction) than through diseases, crimes or accidents." Indeed, there is a wave of suicides by the children of famous writers—a daughter of Schnitzler and a son of Von Hoffmansthal. Klaus' brother Rickey puts a bullet through his heart. And then came Hitler, yet "everybody kept drinking and dancing."

Not long after Hitler met his end, Klaus returned to California to visit his parents; they were then living near Santa Monica. I read in the papers that young Mann had attempted to take his own life, and I wrote him a letter of sympathy and encouragement. In reply, Klaus asked to see me. I cannot recall what stood in the way of an immediate meeting—probably the correction of printer's proofs of a new novel. We put the meeting off, and then Klaus went back to Europe. There he very shortly died. The New York *Times* reported it as "apparent suicide."

* * *

Dr. Erich Fromm, a brilliant contemporary psychiatrist, notes in his book *The Sane Society* the fact that "suicide and alcoholism figures largely coincide." This is not to say that one is always a concomitant of the other; rather, Dr. Fromm questions whether they may not both be "pathological ways of escape from boredom"—the boredom of a society which satisfies our material needs, but little else.

Such a society, I have often felt, exists in Hollywood's movie colony, where life is artificially portrayed and artificially lived. Competition is fierce, the strains of the pace are continual, and the atmosphere is a strange mixture of adulation, sham, exhibitionism, and intrigue.

In Pasadena we live less than an hour's drive from several major studios, and I have seen a great deal of "the industry." Once I wrote a novel which had nothing to do with labor, management or world politics, and Metro-Goldwyn-Mayer bought it for twenty thousand dollars and assigned their top producer, Irving Thalberg, to film it. *The Wet Parade* was its title, and Prohibition was its theme. This was the period when everybody was either a "dry" or a "wet"; my approach to the question was to write a story based on my experiences in the Weisiger house of my childhood.

Thalberg's intention was to hold the balance even between the drys and the wets, and this he succeeded in doing. Robert Young, then beginning his long career, played the juvenile role; Walter Huston portrayed the drunken father; Lewis Stone was featured in it; and Jimmy Durante acted the part of a Prohibition agent with his customary verve. I had never seen this gifted comedian before, and found him delightful.

But when it came to other stories for MGM's cameras, Thalberg and I could not agree; even all these years later, I still cannot shift my focus from the pressing problems of this world to the lighter demands of the screen. And so I have been for the most part an observer of Hollywood life; a deeply interested, emotionally-involved observer, however, for some of the stories I have seen unfold in the movie colony have had dear friends playing tragic roles.

Horace Liveright was one of my friends in the world of letters who came to Hollywood to make pictures. He had been my publisher in New York, and I knew him as one of the kindest of men, equally generous and helpful to young writers and to those who had met with success. He was universally loved; his presence at a dinner table meant wit and erudition and cheer. In Hollywood, however, it also meant too much whiskey.

Here is how Ben Hecht tells Horace's story in his auto-biography, *A Child of the Century:*

> Though he seemed to do nothing but pursue women and drink himself into nightly comas, Liveright was actually a hard worker and a brilliant one. He published scores of fine books and produced a number of successful plays. He loaned courage and money to many fumbling talents. He fought ably against censorship and was one of the chief forces that freed the literature of the Republic from the strangle hold of its old maids. He launched the Modern Library—the first introduction to the larger public of the world's fine writing. There was in New York no more popular and exciting figure than Liveright. Beauty, success and admiration attended him like a faithful retinue, and hundreds of hangers-on were proud to boast of his friendship.
>
> I was in Hollywood some ten years later when

Beatrice Kaufman, who had once worked as a reader in the Liveright firm, telephoned with the news that Horace was dead. He had died (in New York) broke and full of debts.

"I wonder if you could come to his funeral," Beatrice said. "I've been on the phone all day. So far I've only gotten six people to agree to come."

I was unable to leave Hollywood. On a drizzly day, Beatrice Kaufman and five other New Yorkers accompanied the forgotten pauper, Horace Liveright, to his grave.

Now let me finish the story for you. I was in New York City at that time, and was asked to speak at the funeral. I was to Horace's virtues very kind, and to his faults a little blind, and I hoped that at least I was bringing some comfort to his sorrowing old mother. Theodore Dreiser was another of the small band at the burial; and afterwards, we walked down Lexington Avenue together, recalling both the melancholy and the marvelous moments of Liveright's life. Dreiser and Horace had once quarreled bitterly, but all that was forgiven and forgotten. Now I told Dreiser of the dinner parties I had attended with Horace in Hollywood—how he grew drunker and drunker with every course, and we wondered at the way in which, step by step, he had come to this lonely end.

Hollywood's drinking habits have begun to get into books. Not books like this one, but rather in the memoirs of rollicking men who on occasion find a whiskey-filled evening delightful fun. One such work is Gene Fowler's *Minutes of the Last Meeting*, which details the drinking bouts of Sadakichi Hartmann, John Barrymore, and others. Fowler devotes another volume only to Barrymore—certainly one of the finest actors of our time, but without doubt the industry's most maniacal drunkard. His estimate was that in forty years he consumed 640 barrels of hard liquor.

Barrymore earned $375,000 in one year, yet died a bankrupt. Before his death, both Gene Fowler and Ben Hecht attempted to raise funds for the payment of their friend's ever-mounting medical expenses. Yet not one producer, not one director, not one millionaire movie mogul came forward with so much as a dollar for this fallen prince. I have never read a more terrifying picture of the last days of an alcoholic than appears in thirteen appalling pages about Barrymore in *A Child of the Century.*

Douglas Fairbanks was another screen idol whose life ended in tragedy. As much as did any boy in the audience, I as an adult enjoyed watching his fabulous athletic stunts on the screen. And when I met him "in person," as motion picture fans put it, I found him good company. Doug's headquarters was the United Artists studio on Santa Monica Boulevard, and I used to drop in there and watch him work.

Once, during a break between scenes, I told him the story of *The Millennium,* which I had first written as a play and then made into a novel. It was a satiric piece about what the world would be like in another hundred years if we went on as we were headed. In it I let my fancies roam, and I predicted radio broadcasting complete, for example, even before the wireless was discovered. In it I had an airplane flying around the world in twenty-four hours. Now, as I write, jets cross the continent in hours.

Doug expressed delight at the ideas in *The Millennium,* and we began sketching outlines for a picture. But I soon discovered that he was interested only in the gadgets; the satire which I had made the heart of my story was entirely over his head. He was still a little boy who had made the mistake of growing up.

Life had to be lived on his terms, or life wasn't worth living. And his terms called for kings and queens; it demanded action and adventure. He enjoyed telling stories about the potentates with whom he associated. Gossip about John Doe out on a binge meant nothing to Doug, but amusing stories about the dissipations of King Alfonso of Spain he could tell and elaborate with the utmost pleasure. He had reaped colossal success in the world of tangible things—five million dollars net from a single picture, *Robin Hood*. He was perfectly fitted to a world which he had partially created for himself, and which had partially been created for him by press agentry, adulation, and the writers of his swashbuckling roles.

In sum, he couldn't bear to see himself as anything but the all-conquering hero who escaped from a thousand enemies and then overcame them in the final scene. Doug had married America's sweetheart, and the pair reigned as the crowned heads of the industry. All their world was a stage, and all the players had to fit particular roles: the clown had to laugh, the queen had to be gracious, the hero had to be debonair.

But this isn't the way the world works. One does not remain America's leading juvenile forever; cocktails may help one regain the feeling, but not the fact. Lacking inner resources, he was lonely wherever he went. He would turn up somewhere at the ends of the earth after bolting away from Hollywood without notice. He took to chasing other women; he spent a hundred thousand dollars on a single brief yacht cruise. He couldn't bear the fact that his son had become an actor and made a success in his name. He couldn't even endure the fact that his son grew up to be a taller man than he.

His restless searching could find no happiness; his marriage came to an end. His drinking increased. And at fifty-six, according to his niece, he was "a dissipated old man." Then another Hollywood heart suddenly gave out.

Douglas Fairbanks, Jr. spends much of his life in England, where he has been accorded high honors by a real royal family. I, too, have a connection with that family, as odd as anything in royal history could be. Some pages back I mentioned in just a line or two a childhood pillow-fight which might well have changed the whole history of Britain's ruling dynasty. Now I'll tell the tale more completely.

It starts in Old Virginia, where my Uncle Powhatan Montague was raised to become a drinking Southern gentleman. Pow was blessed with two lovely daughters, and one of them—Lelia—was my favorite childhood playmate. Despite our childish romps, one of which ended in a pitched battle (turning Lelia into a panting, half-suffocated, purple-faced little girl), she grew into an intelligent, warm-hearted beauty. Lelia married General George Barnett, who commanded the United States Marine Corps in the Battle of Belleau Wood in 1918, and they settled in Washington.

In nearby Baltimore lived a niece, Wallis Warfield, who was in "reduced circumstances," as the polite phrase puts it. Lelia took charge of the girl, and launched her in Washington society. Wallis was bright and charming; and soon, in the tradition of our family, she married a naval officer.

Meanwhile, a young man who had won the heart of the world as the Prince of Wales became the reigning King of Great Britain. He—like Doug Fairbanks—wanted to remain young. He too refused to face the fact that he had grown middle-aged. He ruled the whole British Empire, but could not quite rule himself.

He was known, biographer Iles Brody tells us, as "a

brandy man." When he became King, his ministers were concerned, and cast about to find some noble lady who might
charm him and keep him from "meddling in the government." But the King had ideas of his own; he preferred the
lady from Baltimore. She was now Mrs. Simpson, having
divorced her first husband and married a second. The King
wanted her for his wife, and she saw nothing wrong in his
plan, even though the established Church of England forbids
remarriage after one divorce, to say nothing of two!

Soon the world learned of the romance; and then when
word leaked out that Prime Minister Baldwin was planning
to force the King to abdicate, there ensued a veritable atomic
explosion of gossip. And what was going on at this time in
Buckingham Palace?

I quote from the December 21, 1936 issue of *Time* magazine: "So much brandy and soda was continually taken by
His Majesty during the early stage of the crisis... that the
work of the Prime Minister was really of heart-breaking difficulty. It was necessary once to apply the stomach pump.
(On Dec. 4, by Lord Horder, the King's physician . . .)"

Edward abdicated, and became the Duke of Windsor.
He married the woman he loved, and made her Duchess. A
well-informed friend in England writes me that "Wallis is
credited with effecting the reform"; and this, of course, I
am happy to record. In so doing she is following in the foot-
steps of the women of the family — but achieving greater
success than my mother had with my father, or Aunt Lelia
Sinclair with my Uncle Arthur, or Aunt Lelia Montague
with Wallis's Great-uncle Pow.

When the news got out that this Great-uncle Pow had
been Upton Sinclair's Uncle Pow, the Hearst newspapers paid
me a thousand dollars to write what I knew about that Baltimore family, its traditions and ways of life. I won't

bore you with the details, but will tell one amusing effect this assignment had on my Cousin Lelia, who had lived (despite our warfare with pillows) to train and guide a woman able to charm a King off his throne.

After a surgical operation, she was lying in a hospital bed when a copy of the Washington Hearst newspaper was brought to her. The front page was given up to but two stories. One was about Edward's abdication, headed by a large picture of Wallis. The other — my story telling about our family — featured a picture of me.

Before Lelia could get over her excitement at this sight, a troop of doctors entered the room to examine her surgical wound. Lelia, who has a delightful sense of fun, held up the paper to them, announcing, "One of these persons is my first cousin, and the other is my niece."

She saw the doctors glance at one another, and she could read perfectly what was in their thoughts: Fever and delirium? Or a psychological case?

13

DR. ROBERT C. CABOT, a scientist impartially investigating the effects of alcohol on people, has written: "Alcohol is always a narcotic, never a stimulant."

Never a stimulant! And yet, all throughout the history of world literature, one comes upon instances of poets and writers turning to wine and whiskey for inspiration, for new thoughts, for "stimulation."

I want to tell you the story of two such poets of our time. Each of them blazed with genius; each was a meteor, here and then gone almost moments later; each was an alcoholic.

The authors of *A History of American Poetry* make this statement about the first: "Of all the poets who came into prominence during the 1930's in America, none is more likely to achieve immortality than Harold Hart Crane."

I think we must add a line from another critic, however.

In *Modern American Poetry*, Louis Untermeyer declares: "There will be those who will find Crane's poetry not merely tangential but cryptic. The difficulty is caused by his combination of allusiveness and allegory, especially since the allusions are often remote and the allegorical symbols personal to the point of privacy."

For the most part, I confess, I am one of those who find Crane's writings cryptic. In my home I have a sumptuous volume entitled *The Limits of Art*. It is essentially an anthology of the world's great literature, collected by Huntington Cairns, a Washington lawyer. It is fastidious and exclusive, and no living writer is represented in the main body of it. At the end are two lines from "The Bridge" by Hart Crane, the only modern poet represented in the 1,400 pages. They are literally the anthologist's "last word":

> *O Thou steeled Cognizance whose leap commits*
> *The agile precincts of the lark's return.*

Perhaps you will puzzle over these lines as long as I have. Or perhaps, as Untermeyer suggests, you will look for clues to Crane's symbolism in the story of his life. It is a record, says his biographer, Brom Weber, which "vibrates with an explosive terror... elated, wretched, violent, Rabelaisian."

His poetry began to appear in "little" magazines and radical publications before he was twenty. He committed each thought to paper; his introspective notes were voluminous; his published letters fill a book some 426 pages long, and they detail his passions and his prejudices with almost unequalled thoroughness.

You read these letters, and find that as a youth Crane's taste in poetry ran to Beaudelaire, Poe, Rimbaud — men whose lives were debauched and despair-ridden. You find him voicing the usual "young highbrow" criticisms of those whose poetry is understandable: Tennyson is dismissed, Elizabeth

Barrett Browning is waved away with a shrug. I think of "Ulysses," and I recall the poem about the great god Pan, how he sat by the river and cut a reed to make a flute — "making a poet out of a man" — and I wince at Crane's callow feelings of superiority.

You read further into his letters; and if you knew him, or knew any of his friends, you realize that the letters do not exaggerate. At the age of twenty he has a job in a drugstore in Akron, Ohio. He hates the town and writes to a friend: "Akron has afforded me one perfect evening, however. I got dreadfully drunk on dreadful raisin brew. . ." He travels, and everywhere he goes his experiences are described in terms of new kinds of drinks. He moves to Cleveland, working for his father, and he writes: "Last night I got drunk on some sherry." He comes to New York, and reports: "There is wine, but what is wine when you drink it alone?" He goes to the country and there comes "an omnibus-full of people from New York and a case of gin, to say nothing of jugs of marvelous hard cider." He dances, "all painted up like an African cannibal." He goes to the airport to meet a man; they miss each other, and by the time they meet, "I had about finished a half pint of alcohol which I had brought for our mutual edification, and he had completely emptied a quart of Bacardi, also originally intended as a mutual benison." He goes on to a long description of a night in a speakeasy from which he was turned out at midnight, being "both reeling but refractory." Some men start slugging him, and he puts up a fight, but is not "in much condition." He is robbed of all his money. Then later we find him with "backache and confinement to the bed. . . But the more probable cause of *that* however is liquor and the cogitations and cerebral excitements it threw me into."

By this time his own poetry has begun to appear, and

critics term it extraordinary. Often in the past he has been poor and hungry; but now there is a stroke of great fortune, and he is able to write to his mother as follows:

"You have probably heard of the banker, Mr. Otto H. Kahn, who has kept the Metropolitan Opera and various other artistic ventures endowed for years. After an interview with Mr. Kahn at his home at 1100 Fifth Avenue, I was given the sum of two thousand dollars to expend on my living expenses during the next year, which time is to be spent in writing the most creative messages I have to give, regardless whether it is profitable in dollars and cents or not."

Hart Crane is twenty-six when this endowment is given him; but his illness of mind and spirit do not disappear with reward and recognition. We find him next in the Isle of Pines, getting drunk and staying drunk on Bacardi, and quarreling with his landlady. Then we find him in Mexico.

He is thirty-three now, and has become a confirmed and hopeless alcoholic; but like so many alcoholics, he denies it. He writes, "I am not, as you surmise, in a constant Bacchic state. Not by any means. However, I happen to be in something approximating it at this moment as I have got to work on the first impressive poem I've started on in the last two years."

Then, a somewhat comical development: he employs a Mexican servant who also takes the liberty of getting drunk. "Senor Daniel Hernandez is morose and very threatening indeed in spite of the fact that I haven't even reprimanded him for his recent drunkenness. Liza is scared to death of him," and so on. . . "Daniel will probably come lurching in about eight tonight and begin to flirt a knife and pistol about. Such is quiet life in this pretty retreat!"

He has got himself a lady, and he writes to her as follows: "Dearest: I was so tremulous and distracted with the domestic situation that I described yesterday to you, that last night I went on a mild tare (sic) with Liza here in the salon. I finally came to the decision of packing up and leaving for the States within the week." Then, "Daniel came home stewed again last night... But I was too gay with Liza and tequila and dancing." Then, five days later, "True to my word last night I got very lit. Daniel had come home that way anyhow, and I took the opportunity to talk to him about sobriety — meanwhile pouring him glass after glass of the Tenampa I bought."

You won't wish to leave Mexico without saying a goodbye to "Senor Daniel Hernandez." Hart writes to his stepmother on April 22nd, "Then at the last moment my servant got roaring drunk and left, and came back and shook the gate to its foundations, yelling threats against my life, terrorizing us for days, until we had to call on the American Embassy for special police service, etc., and so on. Do you wonder that I have been anxious to get off as soon as possible?"

And then, his last communication, number 405. It is dated Havana, Cuba, April 26, 1932: a postcard, saying, "Off here for a few hours on my way north. Will write soon." From that steamer, when the noon whistle blew, he dove into the Caribbean sea and his body was never found.

His great work, an attempt at an epic poem on America, was left incomplete.

There is a line in Wordsworth's poem, "Resolution and Independence," which reads:

. . . *mighty poets in their misery dead* . . .

Such is the epitaph one might utter for Dylan Marlais Thomas, born in October, 1914, dead after his thirty-ninth year. In many ways he was the Byron of our generation — a tempestuous, vibrant young man hailed by colleagues and critics alike as one of the greatest poets of the twentieth century. Like Byron, he became a legend while yet alive. People who had never read a line of his poetry nevertheless knew of his grotesque exploits; they feasted on them and gossiped about them, and asked each other, "What can you expect from so rare a genius?"

Indeed, I have sometimes wondered if Thomas's demented actions did not serve to increase his audience in England and America for his poetry, his dramatic readings, his broadcasts, and later his recordings. People seem to expect and applaud wild amorality from poets.

Thomas was born in Wales, worked briefly as a journalist, and then devoted his full energies to poetry; with imagery that derives both from the ages-old, peaceful fishing villages of his home and the world of twentieth century man, his work has a force and vitality that has affected the whole world of letters. Like Crane, he is often cryptic and puzzling.

Like Crane's, his life is a record of horror and catastrophe.

Thomas was invited to make an American lecture tour by John Malcolm Brinnin, leader of an active poetry center in New York. The story of his four trips is told in Brinnin's *Dylan Thomas in America,* and it is at once shocking and sordid, pathetic and searing. Brinnin meets Thomas at the airport, and the poet goes straight to a bar for a breakfast of double Scotch and soda. He arrives at his hotel room and orders beer. He changes clothes and heads for a Third Avenue bar. Then he goes from bar to bar until he finds a satisfactory one, and there settles down for a succession of beers and a sandwich. His evening is spent in Greenwich Village pub-crawling.

Brinnin has not known him more than a day when he makes this observation:

> He had drunk too fast and too much and while by now I needed no further evidence of his incredible capacity, I could see that he was feeling the effects of this evening's bout more sharply than those of any other since he had arrived. His chin fell onto his chest ... and he slept until his cigarette burned his fingers, jerking him awake. . .

The "purest lyrical poet of the twentieth century —" here he was, sadly crumpled in drunken exhaustion, "Black-tongued and tipsy from Salvation's bottle," unable to think for himself, to face himself, or to face for what they were the insatiable attentions that could only destroy him.

At parties he made direct and uninhibited overtures to women; he was obscene, and delighted in the use of nasty words and shocking phrases. One "morning after" he said to his hostess: "I expect I was a pretty bad boy last night, wasn't I?" She reassured him, saying that "he was fine." "No, I wasn't," he said, "and do you know what the trouble is? I'm going to do the very same thing tonight."

His tour was a fantasy of missed appearances, muddled appointments, drunken binges, boorish behavior — and beauty. His dramatic readings were triumphant. The legend grew.

People thronged to hear him; others thronged to the bars he habituated, to *see* him, like so many curious gazing in excitement at the scene of a wreck or an explosion or a fire. The doctors told him that to drink was to die, but he drank. And he seemed to know what was happening, what he was doing to himself.

In the *Reporter* magazine, Mary Ellin Barrett told the story of one luncheon meeting with Thomas. She had been assigned by *Time* magazine to interview the poet. They meet:

We shook hands. "I am feeling," Thomas informed me, "like death. A bad night. A very bad night . . . Let's get a drink."

They go to a nearby restaurant. Thomas has a drink; then his wife comes in, saying that she has been looking for him in three bars already. He orders oysters and another Tom Collins.

The reporter tries hard to get him to answer the questions she has prepared. She has copied out eight lines from a poem which she could not understand, and she asks him to explain them. One line reads, "Be ye sure the Thief will seek a way sly and sure." She wants to know what "the Thief" symbolizes.

"The Thief?" he said, quietly, "Who is the Thief? Well, today for me the Thief is this." He pointed to his empty glass. "Alcohol is the Thief today."

There is terror in stories like these; terror at what whiskey can do to the minds of men. And there is poignancy, and sorrow for the sufferer unable to break from the grip. People who knew Thomas, even those who knew him only through his work, felt shock — and then sympathy. Here is the way Hans Meyerhoff described one such experience in "The Violence of Dylan Thomas," an article which appeared in the July 11, 1955, issue of *The New Republic*:

I saw and heard Dylan Thomas only once. *De mortuis* . . . Perhaps it is unbecoming to remember him as I do. . .

It was a public reading of poetry at a university . . . He had trouble finding his bearings behind the lectern. He appeared unsteady, nervous, and ill at ease. The notes from which he was going to read were written on loose sheets which looked like scraps of paper. As he was shuffling them rapidly, perhaps to put them into some kind of order, they fluttered to the floor. He stooped down, scrambled after them, and scooped them up in awkward gestures — all the while cursing in *sotto voce* obscenities. Then he poured himself a glass of water; only he didn't. He held the water pitcher with an outstretched arm and aimed at the glass below; but he missed it; and a steady stream of water ran from the pitcher onto the floor. There was no doubt now that he was unsteady. Nobody laughed. There was a deep silence in the room.

Then he began to read, without a word of greeting, from his notes. He read hurriedly and half-audibly, as if embarrassed.... Let's get this over with as quickly as possible, because I am suffering — he seemed to say and said it in almost these words. And then the initial shock gave way to a wave of deep sympathy among his listeners; for he obviously *was* suffering. This was some kind of indignity; and he responded to it with ill-concealed disdain and suppressed anger. Let's get this over with quickly so that I can read a poem. For when he reached for the books on his side, he was a being transformed...

Dylan Thomas died suddenly, in the midst of his 1953 lecture tour. A group of friends and admirers took up a collection for his wife and children.

Mighty poets in their misery dead!

14

The liquor industry spends approximately $250,000,000 a year to advertise and promote its products, and additional millions of dollars on "educational" work. The liquor lobby is in every state capitol and in our national capitol; it has card files of executives and legislators. The lobby knows who its friends are, and it seeks to hold them. It knows who its enemies are, and it seeks to convert or defeat them.

The lobbies have several purposes. Always, of course, to fight against Prohibition movements and to campaign for lower taxes on liquors. They insist that they are four-square against drunkenness. Moderation is what they preach. Alcoholism is a "disease" they deplore.

Alcoholism *is* a disease, of course. But it scarcely seems to me that this excuses or clears the distillers of responsibility. Cancer does not advertise itself as a symbol of "thoughtful hospitality"; heart disease does not spend a quarter of a billion dollars annually to announce that it is an "aid to gracious living." Neither polio nor tuberculosis describe themselves in handsome posters and colorful magazine-spreads as a means to healthful relaxation and enjoyment. *The Brewers Digest* once discussed the sales condition of the beer industry, and reached the conclusion that it "had not yet found a satisfactory answer to the problem of introducing beer to a high percentage of the younger generation." *Other* diseases are not sold, advertised, pressured, promoted, lobbied and press-agented in this way. Other diseases are fought with drastic surgery or skilled preventive medicine.

I have come to a point in this book, I believe, where I must for a time depart from my stories about my friends and fellows in the world of writing. With you I want to look at facts and statistics about liquor; the chemistry of its effects, the extent of its damage and the cost of its depredations. With you I want to look at the record of youthful drinking in our nation today. These were the facts which impelled me to write this book; they frighten me, and they rouse in me a desire to fight with the weapon I know best — truthful words.

There are more than four and a half million alcoholics in this nation today, and almost three-quarters of a million of them are women. This is the figure given us by the Yale University Center of Alcoholic Studies. It is a figure for the year 1953, arrived at in the last month of 1955; but there is no reason for us to believe that the number of alcoholics decreased during the long months while the statistics were gathered.

Indeed, every indication presented in the study is that the number today must be far higher. The percentage of alcoholics per 100,000 Americans increased only slightly between 1952 and 1953; but between 1940 and 1952, it increased by *forty-five percent* among males and *fifty-two percent* among females.

Notice that these figures are based on population — so that when one reads that there are 7,800 alcoholics in Washington, D. C., for every 100,000 people, it means that there are 7,800 alcoholics in a group of people which includes newborn babies, grade-school children, young teen-agers, adults who abstain completely, and finally the adults who drink. The figure of concern to me is how many of these adults who are "social drinkers" and "moderate drinkers" become alcoholics — because that's the way my father and his brothers began, and that's what Jack London and George Sterling thought they were, and what Hart Crane and Dylan Thomas hoped to be: "social drinkers."

The answer to my question comes from Dr. Andrew Ivy, professor of the Department of Physiology of the University of Illinois. Reporting the results of investigations made by the Institute of Scientific Studies for the Prevention of Alcoholism, Dr. Ivy declared that one out of every sixteen casual, social, moderate drinkers becomes an alcoholic; one out of nine becomes what he calls a "problem drinker." He went on to express the fear that should the present rate of increase in alcohol consumption and alcoholism continue, the ratio of the "problem" drinker to the "social drinker" will similarly increase within ten or fifteen years from one in nine to *one in five*.

Alcoholism is now the nation's fourth most serious health problem. Science has begun to find ways to treat it with a variety of weapons: vitamins and hormones to restore the body balance, drugs to decrease the pressure of psychological difficulties, other drugs to keep the alcoholic from going back to the bottle by making him violently ill if he "falls off the wagon," and psychotherapy to get at the emotional reasons for his urge to destroy himself with whiskey. Each day there are new studies of why liquor "gets at" some people more than others: it is a chemical imbalance, one school says. It is an allergy, says the next faction.

It is even made plain that in truth no one who drinks escapes ill effects. The December, 1953, issue of *Scientific American* magazine featured an article by Leon A. Greenberg, associate professor and director of the Department of Applied Physiology at Yale University. He is one of the founders of the Yale Center of Alcohol Studies, and the inventor of the Alcometer, the device by which the police tell whether you are High, Tight, or Drunk. There could be no better authority.

Dr. Greenberg tells us that alcohol is not digested, but passes directly into the bloodstream. When it reaches the brain, this is what happens:

A blood concentration of about .05 per cent of alcohol, which in a person of average size results from drinking two or more ounces of whiskey, depresses the uppermost level of the brain — the center of inhibitions, restraint and judgment. At this stage the drinker feels that he is sitting on top of the world; he is "a free human being"; many of his normal inhibitions vanish; he takes personal and social liberties as the impulse prompts; he is long-winded and can lick anybody in the country. Such a man has undergone an obvious blunting of self-criticism.

Double that amount, and the drinker begins to stagger. Professor Greenberg tells us:

Contrary to old and popular belief, alcohol does not stimulate the nervous system. The illusion of stimulation results from the removal of inhibitions and restraints. The effects may be compared to a releasing of the brakes, not a stepping on the accelerator. Even with a few drinks, digital dexterity is reduced; auditory and visual discrimination fall away; tactile perception is lowered; the speed of motor response drops. Despite these measurable losses, the drinker often asserts that his reaction, perception and discrimination are better.

This is the false effect, then, which has led so many writers to believe that their work is more fluent and inspired after a round of drinks. Like "peace gestures" from a warring nation, whiskey's first false glow succeeds in making even shrewd and trained observers let down their guard. They recognize the eventual danger, yet want to believe the present propaganda. Here, for example, is the way Stanley Walker expressed his thoughts on drinking in his book, *City Editor*:

In the popular mind, a newspaper man is one who drinks a great deal. It is true that most newspaper men drink; it is also true that booze takes many of them to a pathetic ending. But the majority of newspaper men today are careful about their liquor; they have to be . . . the stories of reporters who write just as well on twelve highballs as when cold sober are utter bunk. A man may stagger horribly through writing a column while groggy and get by with it, but he would have done much better if he had had nothing to drink.

All industry is now awakening to the fact that people indeed do "much better" when sober. Professor Greenberg and his colleagues at Yale report that the alcoholic worker is absent from his job an average of twenty-five days a year; that while *on* the job, his accident rate is double that of the

normal employee. Current estimates are that alcoholic workers and employees with "hangovers" cost industry one billion
dollars a year in money and 400,000,000 man-hours of time.
Every day of the week, some 175,000 men and women are
absent from work because of what they drank the night before.

And do you want the picture of other costs of drunkenness? Here in my state, it was announced that the cost of
liquor-caused traffic casualties was over $36,500,000 in Los
Angeles alone. In Massachusetts, they studied the relationship between the amount of money received as revenue income from the sale of liquor, and money paid out because of
alcoholism; and they found that for every one dollar of liquor
revenue coming to the state treasury, the taxpayers paid out
$4.82 to take care of known liquor-caused court cases, jail
costs, hospitalization, emergency care on highways, and wel-
fare work.

One final set of figures: in 1953, when — according to
Yale University — there were 4,589,000 alcoholics in this nation, our national consumption of liquor was reckoned at
18.95 gallons *per person*, thus reaching the staggering total of
3,002,000,000 gallons.

I reflect on all these figures, and in truth I would expect
to find a nation united against the glamorizing of drinking.
Instead, I read in one of our smart magazines an account of
two days spent with one of our most eminent novelists. I
learned in the reading of it that the gentleman desires either
bourbon or champagne every hour or two, and certainly devotes a good part of his conversation to the flavors and quali-
ties of these liquors. In another publication, one of our most
widely-circulated weekly magazines, there was an account of
a second respected and eminent novelist. I quote a part of
one sentence, with the permission of the magazine writer:

"He escapes periodically and sometimes for periods of weeks into alcoholism, until his drinking has become legendary in his town and in his profession, and hospitalization and injections have on occasion been necessary to save his life."

I read these reports, and I wonder what the reaction of our youth will be as they peruse them. Will they feel, as did the Lamb hero, that one must burn the house to its foundations in order to roast a pig? Will they feel that the pathway to genius is through gin?

Just what *is* the pathway our youth is following?

Look with me, if you will, into a book which gives many of the answers. It is titled *Drinking in College*, and was written by Robert Straus and Selden D. Bacon, who based their report on research conducted by Yale University.

The sub-title of the work is "A Survey of the Customs and Attitudes Toward Alcohol of Men and Women in Twenty-seven American Colleges." The flaps of the book's dust jacket express its contents clearly:

This is the long-awaited report of the survey conducted by the Yale Center of Alcoholic Studies on the drinking customs and attitudes of college students in the United States. From 1949 through 1951, seventeen thousand men and women students in twenty-seven colleges provided information about their social background and personal habits and attitudes toward liquor... Here at last is an organized body of factual knowledge to replace speculation, to provide a basis for a realistic explanation of behavior, and to suggest more reasonable and realistic action by persons... who are called upon to make important decisions and provide guidance for young people.

College students are a group of particular significance for the study of drinking. They are at the age when drinking starts for many persons, initial experiences are fresh in their minds, and they easily identify the pressures and purposes associated with early drinking. This study shows who drinks and who does not, when and where those who drink first started drinking, why and how much they drink, the influence of parents and the significance of income, religious affiliation, and ethnic background.

The basic mass figure is: seventy-four percent of all the 17,000 students "reported having used alcoholic beverages to some extent." The chapters of the book report on various aspects of the problem, and I quote a few of the figures:

Chapter Four: Seventy-nine percent of the men who drink and sixty-five percent of the women who drink report that their drinking started before entering college.

Chapter Six: *"Drinking Parents."* Two-thirds of the fathers drink, and so do forty-eight percent of the mothers.

Chapter Seven: *"What do Students Drink?"* As first preference, the answer is: for men, forty-seven percent beer, eleven percent wine, forty-two percent spirits. For women the choices are: seventeen percent beer, twenty-five percent wine, and fifty-eight percent spirits.

Chapter Eight: *"How Much and How Often?"* Frequency during the past year, one to five times: for men, nineteen percent; for women, twenty-seven percent.

Twice a month to once a week: for men, thirty-six percent; for women, thirty-seven percent. Four or more days a week: for men, three percent; for women, one percent.

Chapter Nine: *"When, Where, with Whom?"* We

learn that of students who drink, eleven percent of the men and nine percent of the women began drinking between the ages of eleven and fifteen. Thirty-six percent of the men and forty-seven percent of the women began in their sixteenth or seventeenth years. Fifty-three percent of the men and forty-four percent of the women began at eighteen and older.

Chapter Ten: *"High, Tight, and Drunk."* "Tight" is defined as "Unsteadiness in ordinary physical activities, or noticeable aggressiveness, or over-solicitousness, or loss of control over social amenities or of verbal accuracy, or slight nausea." Twenty percent of the men and fifty-one percent of the women report that they have never been tight. Twenty-five percent of the men and thirty-two percent of the women report that they have been tight from one to five times. Eighteen percent of the men and nine percent of the girls report being tight from six to fifteen times; seventeen percent of the men and four percent of the girls, from sixteen to fifty times. For from fifty-one to one hundred times, the percentage of women is negligible and that of men is five percent. Finally, four percent of the men report being "tight" a hundred times or more; and eleven percent of the men and four percent of the women report having been tight "at times," but do not state the frequency.

And then comes the table reporting on those who have been *drunk,* which is defined as "an overstepping of social expectancies (short of completely passing out), loss of control in ordinary physical activities, and inability to respond to reactions of others." Thirty-eight percent of the men and eighty-two percent of the women report that this has occurred once; and eight percent of the men and one percent of the women report that it occurred from six to ten times. Beyond that the percentage of women is again negligible, but five percent of the men report having been drunk from eleven to twenty times, and four percent of the men and one percent of the women report that on occasion they "have been drunk," but do not state the frequency.

And then the most advanced stage, *passing out*. The number of those who report this as having happened "once" is sixteen percent for men, seven percent for women. "Twice" is eight percent for men, one percent for women. More than twice, one percent of women drinkers and nine percent of the men.

The book reveals that seventy-nine percent of the men and sixty-five percent of the women had their first drink before entering college. With regard to parental drinking, ninety-two percent of the men report that both of their parents used alcohol; eighty-three percent of the women report the same.

I invite all parents to examine the statement which follows: "When both parents drink, eighty-three percent of the female students are drinkers, compared with a mere twenty- three percent when both parents abstain. These data suggest that parental example is a factor of major significance in drinking by young people."

Remember, then, that seventy-four percent of our college youth are now "social" and "moderate" drinkers. Imagine that one of every sixteen of them will be an alcoholic. Remind yourself that one out of every five or nine will be a "problem drinker." You will go with these facts to the young people you know, and you will warn them and plead with them.

And I can tell you now what many will say: "But drinking is a *custom*. Everybody in my fraternity (sorority, class) does it. If you don't, you're a freak!"

Fortunately, the authors of *Drinking in College* delved into this problem as well. And Table 95 in their book, headed

"Attitude Toward Abstainers," tells quite clearly what happens to one socially if he does not drink in college.

If the student abstains, and makes no special point about it, fifty-four percent of his fellow-students will have feelings of admiration, approval and respect for him. Forty percent will be indifferent to his position. Four percent will feel resentment, scorn, disapproval or derogation. Two percent will feel pity.

Thus, among every ten of his classmates, there will be nine who either do not care or feel real admiration for the student who does not drink. Just one will feel scorn or pity.

And what about the girl who abstains from liquor? In this case, thirty-two percent of her fellow-students will not care at all. Sixty-two percent will admire, approve and respect her. And again, four percent will feel hostility; and two percent, pity. Almost two-thirds of the women will think the *better* of the girl who does not drink!

These are the figures which the brewers and the distillers fear! These are the figures which make them spend a quarter of a billion dollars a year to show that liquor is essential to social success. This is why their sales managers and their salesmen, their advertising experts and their publicists, their copywriters and their artists deem it important to introduce their product "to a high percentage of the younger generation."

They know that more than half the country admires the men and the women who do not fall for the lies of their advertisements nor the lies of their product.

15

"Old Crow" is the name of a liquor manufactured by the National Distillers Products Corporation. It is available in two proofs — 86-proof and 100-proof. Its advertisements call it: "The Greatest Name in Bourbon."

The brand has been sold in the United States for over one hundred years. This is a source of considerable pride to the distillers, and in magazine advertisements they frequently link their product with other names which have figured in the American past — Daniel Webster, Henry Clay, Mark Twain, Governor Robert Letcher of Kentucky, Bret Harte, and so on.

So great is their interest in the part their bourbon has played in our national heritage that they have set up a New York City office called the "Old Crow Historical Bureau." In advertisments they invite the public "to participate in a search for historical facts about Old Crow." And those fortunate scholars who are the first to contribute an authenticated fact about "The Greatest Name in Bourbon," and have it accepted, receive an award from the company of $250.00.

An advertisement making this generous offer recently appeared in *Saturday Review* magazine. One award-winning fact cited in it referred to Jack London. It told how London brought a bottle of Old Crow as a gift to his friend, Martin Eden, and then proposed a toast: "Skaal to the Old Crow, Martin — it is best!"

Now I cannot vouch for the brands of the liquor he consumed, but I can tell the "Old Crow Historical Bureau" many more interesting facts about Jack's drinking. And I should imagine that in the service of Americana—that in the light of their enthusiasm for "the raw materials of history," as they call these facts — they will want to bring the rest of the story to the American public. My account will certainly demonstrate what a connoisseur of alcohols Jack London was, and thus the story should make his estimate of Old Crow as "the best" all the more impressive.

I pledge that if I am awarded a prize of $250.00, I shall use it to disseminate even further the story of London's experiences with 86-proof and 100-proof drinks. We'll put our heads together, the "Old Crow Historical Bureau" and I, and we'll plan to send reprints to all those places where interested students of alcohol gather — bars, retail liquor stores, certain wards of certain hospitals, prisons, the "skid row" streets of innumerable cities, and so on.

Here, then, is the rest of Jack London's story.

The world cruise of London's ship, *The Snark*, was brought to an end during World War 1 by his ill health. Jack wrote me from Australia to say that he had contracted nine tropical diseases; this seemed a fearsome total, and I wondered if some of the illnesses were not more likely temporary manifestations of too much drink.

Jack had set out for the South Seas with no liquor on board, and with the resolve that he would drink only when in port. But he tells us in his book, *John Barleycorn, or Alcoholic Memoirs*, that such was not long the case. He was soon in port, and soon he drank; then, as the voyage continued, he discovered that a quantity of liquor had been stowed on board without his knowledge. He drained this supply; then when he reached the next port, he wanted more. And after that he always carried liquor on the little vessel.

Ashore, he drank with his guests and with his hosts; at sea he drank alone or with his crew. Then he sold the vessel and returned to the United States by steamship, settling on a ranch he had bought in the Valley of Moon, north of San Francisco. He had written me about it. "A most wonderful place," he said. He was going to plant eucalyptus trees on the ranch and make a fortune. Later he wrote that he had indeed planted a hundred thousand trees, but the fortune never materialized.

He tells us that it was at this ranch that he began hard drinking again. He doesn't know "just why" — but he supposes that he was beginning to pay for his score of years of habitual dallying with John Barleycorn. He makes all sorts of excuses and rationalizations: when guests came to the ranch it would have been a "hardship" for them not to have liquor. So he laid in a supply, telling himself that it was only for his guests — but he drank it himself. He didn't know how to mix cocktails, so he had one of his barkeeper friends in Oakland prepare the cocktails and ship them to him. Then he noticed that even when he didn't have guests he wanted those cocktails.

He goes on to reveal what all drinkers will recognize, the process by which a man is lured into ever greater indulgence. There had been a time when a single cocktail would give him the glow he craved; but now he found he needed two. And if his guest wanted only one, Jack would drink another in secret. When he had no guest he would still drink two.

He says, "And right there John Barleycorn had me. I was beginning to drink regularly. I was beginning to drink alone. And I was beginning to drink, not for hospitality's sake, not for the sake of taste, but for the effect of the drink."

The time came when the two cocktails were not enough; he had to have three. Then three just between the time he ended his morning's work and sat down to eat his noon meal! He takes you along step by step, showing you how an alcoholic is made, and to me it all seemed as familiar as the letters that spell my name.

He would ride over the mountains on horseback, he would swim in his swimming pool, and then he would feel "glorious" — and when could be a more proper time to have a drink than when one is feeling so good, and can feel more glorious still? He would have a crowd of friends over to the ranch, and they would all feel "glorious." Or he would get good news in the mail, and would want to celebrate that.

And sometimes there would be bad news. For example, his favorite horse got caught in a barbed-wire fence and kicked himself to death. The way to get over the grief was to have an extra cocktail. Next there came a whole string of disasters in Jack's agricultural and animal husbandry projects — his registered pigs all died of pneumonia, his prize shorthorn bull fouled a horn and broke its neck, his elaborate new ranch house burned to the ground the day it was finished, sharp traders overcharged him, and spiteful neighbors tied up his water rights. In short, he had a typical run of rancher's hard luck. And when could be a more proper time to have a drink than when one is feeling so miserable, and needs a "lift"? And so he drank constantly. When he went to the city he always ordered double cocktails "because they saved time."

All this continued and grew worse. When he travelled he was afraid he might be stuck somewhere without a drink, so he always carried several quarts with him. He had looked down on people who did that in the past, but now he did it "unblushingly." He cast all rules by the board; he drank alone, and when he was with other people he out-drank them. He says he was carrying an "alcoholic conflagration" around with him. He reached and passed the quart-of-whiskey-a-day mark.

New struggles to control himself began, but he was powerless. He had begun to take a drink in the middle of his morning's work; now he decided that this he should do no more. But when he sat down to the typewriter he made a frightening discovery — no ideas would come *unless* he had a drink. John Barleycorn was holding him up — no drink, no inspiration. He had once told me in New York that he made it a rule to earn a hundred dollars every morning before breakfast; now Jack London would sit at his typewriter and the only idea he could think of was the bottle in the cabinet on the other side of the room. He would go there and get a drink and immediately the ideas would flow, the thousand words were magically tapped out on the typewriter. But they were of ever-deteriorating quality. The year before his last he was seen wandering about the bars of Oakland, dazed and disagreeably drunk.

Can you imagine anything more pitiful than the spectacle of a man of genius wasting his faculties in a struggle such as this? At forty he had reached the pinnacle as the best-known, best-paid, most popular writer in the world. He had scaled this height from difficult, squalid beginnings. The illegitimate child of an itinerant astrologer and an emotionally unstable mother, he was raised in poverty by a loyal and inexhaustibly friendly stepfather and stepsister. Jack had hurtled upwards on the basis of his own unbounded talent, overflowing good spirits, and persevering courage. Think of him as he takes stock of himself: he has everything in the world to make him happy. He has a wife who is devoted to him, an estate which is his dream of loveliness, horses to ride, and a host of friends riding at his side. He has money in the bank and he has fame — his name is known and honored all over the world. But the only thing that's important now is a bottle. Not even a bottle — just a drink!

He knows that whiskey is poison to him; yet he cannot live without that poison. He makes all sorts of resolutions, tries all sorts of devices, but he cannot live without his whiskey: he cannot think, he cannot write. He knows his work is deteriorating. His last novels, *Burning Daylight* and *The Valley of the Moon,* are so poor in quality that you can scarcely believe you are reading books by London. The magazines still buy his tales. The publishers still issue them, because they bear the label. The public will take them. But the writer knows!

When *John Barleycorn* was published, Jack sent me a copy and I wrote to thank him. I praised him for his courage and frankness. But to myself I uttered a private prayer —

that having gone this far in his understanding of the terrible dangers of drink, he would be able to go the one great step further, and give it up completely. I feared the hint of disaster which seemed implicit in his concluding words of *John Barleycorn*. I feared his insistence that he was not an alcoholic, that he was going to continue drinking, "but more skillfully, more discreetly."

Jack's book was a fantastic success, spurred on by widespread activities in its behalf by zealous Prohibitionists. That the work of a drinker who had no intention of stopping drinking should become a major propaganda piece in the campaign for Prohibition is surely one of the choice ironies in the history of alcohol.

Prohibition came closer, but Jack London did not stop drinking. Nor did he drink "more skillfully, more discreetly." George Sterling wrote to tell me how things were going — and they were not going well.

Jack's manners had become those of a nerve-wracked man. He would take over the conversation and pound the table. If you disagreed with him he would quarrel. His lively wit had dulled; his humor was crude horseplay, or crazily complex practical jokes.

He had purchased some trick drinking glasses, which had tiny holes around the rim; when a guest tilted the glass to drink, the liquid would run down his neck. His swimming pool was constructed with a secret passage under the water. Jack would dive in and swim through that passage and come up in another place, leaving his guests terrified, sure that he had drowned. A book bearing the title *A Loud Noise* was left around; when the cover was opened, a firecracker inside exploded. Rope arrangements permitted guests' beds to be rocked from another room; hapless visitors, thus shaken from their beds in the dark of the night, would dash out of their rooms, shouting "Earthquake! Earthquake!" And Jack would laugh: this was humor, this was fun, this was wit.

Even after their long, intimate years of friendship, George Sterling could no longer endure the drunken rituals at the ranch. His visits to London became ever less frequent.

Yet Jack could still show flashes of his former self. He decided to go to Hawaii, and took with him the bulky manuscript of a new book I had written, *The Cry for Justice*. He read it on the steamer, and sent back in the mails one of the finest pieces of writing he ever did. It was an introduction for my book, and I quote from it:

It is so simple a remedy — merely service. Not one ignoble thought or act is demanded by anyone of all the men and women in the world to make fair the world. The call is for nobility of thinking, nobility of doing. The call is for *service*, and such is the wholesomeness of it, he who serves all best serves himself.

In the fall of 1916 he returned to the ranch in the Valley of Moon. Craig told me that she was worried about Jack. "I feel that he's in trouble," she said. "I think you ought go to see him."

But then we read in a newspaper that Jack was dead. At seven a.m. on the morning of the sixteenth of November, he had been found unconscious in his bedroom. Two empty bottles, one with a morphine sulphate label and the other labelled atropine sulphate, were found on the floor, and on a pad there were scribbled calculations of the lethal dosages of the drugs. Doctors treated him all day, but except for a single brief flicker of consciousness he did not respond, and at a little after seven that evening he died.

16

*My husband is going Crusading again. Shall
I go with him?*

*You may guess what Crusading is. It is a
word we have chosen for something he is always
promising not to do — and which he is always
doing...*

I quote these words from *Spring Song*, 1918, a prose
poem written by Craig just a few years after our marriage.
It has been our fortune and our fate to fight side by side in
many crusades; and I would like to share with you both her
words and the story of how she came to write them.

America was at war with Germany; and I, although an
ardent pacifist, had argued for our entry into that war, be-
lieving deeply that this country could not permit the democratic nations to be conquered by the Kaiser. Now my one
hope was to help prevent the anguish of another such conflict

in the future. I resolved to start a monthly magazine to be devoted to "a Clean Peace and the Internation."

Our funds were low, and Craig was straining against heavy obstacles to create a home for us and a studio for me. Revolted by the savagery of the war, she was bending all her efforts to these two domestic goals. My decision to borrow money and publish a monthly periodical seemed more than she could contemplate. But I said it was my duty—and duty is an almost-sacred word to Craig. For several days she wrestled with the problem, and then one morning she silently handed *Spring Song* to me as her first contribution to my new magazine.

> . . . *My husband is going Crusading again.*
> *Shall I go with him?*
> *I sit frowning over endless manuscripts; and then I look out of the window, and oh, it is spring-time out there! I see jonquils, and a breath of them floats to me with the warm sunshine; beyond are the mountains where I know there are "trails," calling for footsteps. Is not my duty there—when all my being yearns for sweet, calm hours under the skies? I am so weary of Crusades! May not this Crusade be deferred—just a little while?*
> *Or is this, as my husband says, the supreme hour for the world, when to act on the call of conscience may be to answer the need of the whole world? Is it, as he says, no time to think of beauty, peace, and health—when young men are going to face the cannon, answering the call of their conscience?*
> *My husband and I are going Crusading together!*

The magazine was launched; it failed to achieve a "clean

peace," of course, just as the League of Nations failed to achieve a lasting peace. The years sped by, the problems of World War I festered and grew—and in the mid-thirties, suddenly but inevitably, there was Hitler. Again I could foresee a world conflagration. Hitler had announced his program, and he was fast implementing it. He was going to seize all of Europe, and he was certain of his power to do it. He called the rest of the world fools, and indeed we were—too foolish to arm, too frightened to say "thus far and no farther," too blindly hopeful to understand the writing on the wall.

I watched events, and was tormented by them; again I was a pacifist predicting a war and calling for it. Tension was heaping up in my soul.

Back in the old home in Pasadena which Craig had made for me—there was a fence and a rose hedge around it now, and it was quiet—I walked up and down one night in the garden path, thinking. Then something happened for which I have no explanation and no name. It was as though a spring had been touched or a button pressed . . .

A novel came rolling into the field of my mental vision; not just the outline, but a whole series of events, with the emotions that accompanied them, a string of characters, old and young, good and bad, rich and poor. I had had this experience before, but never with such force, such mass and persistence. There was no resisting it, and I didn't try. I spent the next thirty-six hours in a state of absorption. I slept little, but lay in bed and "saw" my theme. I ate little and talked little. When I told my wife what was happening, she was delighted, for this meant that I was out of politics and doing "my kind of work." I trod the garden path hard under my feet, and filled sheets of paper with notes of characters, places, events—the whole panorama of a novel called *World's End.*

The scene is Europe, with a visit to New England and New York. The time of the story is 1913 to 1919. I had lived in England, Holland, Germany, France and Italy during 1912 and 1913, and naturally my thoughts had been there during the years of my story, the years of warmaking and peacemaking. Also, the records of the period are voluminous; for that one novel I must have read a hundred books, and to check my information I must have written hundreds of letters and asked a thousand questions.

The hero is Lanny Budd, an American boy, thirteen at the beginning; at a dancing school in Germany he meets a German boy and an English boy, and later we watch all the events of the war and the peace through the eyes of these three. Lanny's father and grandfather are American munitions manufacturers, and so his view is from the inside of affairs. When I was writing about the Paris Peace Conference, I communicated with an authority on modern fiction to find out if anybody had ever used that event in a novel. The reply was, "*Could* anybody?" I thought that somebody "could," and now I have. My account of those events was read and checked by eight or ten gentlemen who were on the American staff.

World's End was published in 1940, and it became a great success; it was taken by a major book club, and its sales have been 200,000 in America and 40,000 in Britain. It has been translated and published in seventeen languages that I know about. Even before I finished, I realized that Lanny would go on. So much had happened in the world—how could he, situated as he was, keep out of it? How could his friends keep out of it?

They couldn't; and so, every year, there was a new Lanny Budd story. Volume III, *Dragon's Teeth*, deals with the coming of the Nazis, and it received the Pulitzer Prize.

And then along came my friend Cornelius Vanderbilt, Jr., who was also a devoted friend to Franklin Roosevelt; he told me what it was like to be a "presidential agent," how it was to go into the White House by the so-called "social door," which is really the back door. So Lanny Budd was taken to President Roosevelt, too, and after that there was nobody in the U.S. or Europe he couldn't meet, and nothing he couldn't find out.

Volume V was *Presidential Agent,* and then later there was *Presidential Mission.* In between these came *A World to Win,* and it was taken by another book club, and more than 750,000 copies were sold. I try to guess why, and my theory is that it happened because there were two young ladies in the story competing for the love of the desirable hero, and the reader was kept guessing as to which one was going to get him.

In this book, I am afraid, there can be no element of suspense. When one of a man's suitors is whiskey, the reader does not have to guess "who is going to get him in the end." I have known many men who drank; they were often men who in other ways kept stern discipline on themselves—so many words to be written every day, so many hours of relaxation, so many hours of research. In this one area of their lives, however, there was no discipline. And gradually, this one area became the *whole* area.

I have known just a few—three men, only two of whom I can name—who reached the stage of "problem drinking" and then stopped. The stories of two I reserve for the next chapter. The third is Eugene O'Neill, the late playwright who almost singlehandedly changed the course of the American theatre.

Eugene O'Neill came of a family of actors; he was a wild boy, and was suspended from Princeton for throwing a beer bottle through a window in Woodrow Wilson's home. He went away to sea, and—to quote the obituary report in *Time* magazine—"His sea voyages were punctuated by Homeric booze-feats ashore, a slum-bum stretch when he lived at Jimmy the Priest's saloon in Manhattan and slept on the hickory-topped tables, too broke to pay $3.00 a month for a room; then he was brought up sharply by an attack of tuberculosis."

I have mentioned the Provincetown Players, organized by George Cram Cook. They produced O'Neill's plays, and their productions rocked the literary and theatrical worlds. I remember seeing *The Emperor Jones* on Broadway, and being hypnotized by it. I remember reading *Moon of the Carribees,* and knowing that we had a real dramatist in our midst. On the other hand, I was dismayed by the muddled symbolism and confused allegory of *The Great God Brown;* and when one of O'Neill's co-workers told me that the playwright went off "on drinking bouts that last two or three weeks, so bad that his friends never know if they will be able to pull him through," I wondered if this were not contributing to the change in his work.

In 1932, George Jean Nathan wrote an affectionate portrait of O'Neill. And in one section of it, he told the story of the dramatist's early drinking habits, and of his eventual decision against liquor. I quote:

> Years ago, he was a drinker of parts. In fact, there were times when he went on benders that lasted a whole month and times when he slept next to the bung-hole of a whiskey barrel at Jimmy the Priest's and when Jimmy, the proprietor, coming to work the next morning, found the barrel one-eighth gone ...
>
> The favorite tipple of the brotherhood, when

one or another of the members—usually O'Neill, who at intervals would contrive to cozen a dollar out of his father—managed in some way to get hold of the price, was, aside from the breakfast rye, Benedictine drunk by the tumberful. But such treats were rare and makeshifts were necessary. Alcohol mixed with camphor was found—after one got used to the taste—to have a pretty effect. Varnish diluted with water was also discovered to have its points. And there were days when even wood alcohol mixed in small doses with sarsaparilla, with just a soupçon of benzine to give it a certain bouquet, was good enough, in the brothers' view, for any man who wasn't a sissy ...

About four or five years ago, however, he hoisted himself onto the water-wagon and has sat thereon with an almost Puritanical splendor and tenacity. Like many another reformed bibber, he now views the wine-cup with a superior dudgeon and is on occasion not averse to delivering himself of eloquent harangues against it and its evils.

O'Neill lived a life of incredible tragedy. He once attempted suicide; he was twice divorced; his daughter Oona was estranged from him; a son committed suicide; his younger son had to be treated for narcotics addiction. He became a victim of Parkinson's, a dreadful disease which combines palsy and rigidity; and although science was finding new drugs while O'Neill lived—drugs which for most victims offered at least some relief and help—he did not respond to any.

All the tragedy of his life is mirrored in his plays; and you can find it all, even the atmosphere of his youthful days on the New York waterfront, in his last major drama, *The Iceman Cometh*. The setting is a saloon like Jimmy the Priest's. The characters are a flophouse assortment from all classes and all parts of the world—a former British army captain, a former leader of a Boer commando group, a circus man, an ex-police lieutenant, two anarchists, a Harvard law-school graduate, three neighborhood tarts, a bartender.

And then there's Hickey, a hardware salesman who has come to urge them to "reform." He sends them out to regain their places in the world outside the saloon, but in the fourth act they all come back defeated, broken, making pathetic excuses for themselves, trying once again to latch onto the "pipe dreams" which make their misery one touch more tolerable. They go back to the bottles which gave them false hope.

It is a shattering play; it offers no hope, no future, no reason for being. You know that once it was O'Neill's world, that he shared these tragedies. You admire the way he firmly refused to go back to the easy delusion of liquor. You can only have pity for the tragedies which nonetheless came to torment him. You can only wish that he found hope and understanding before he died.

Not drinking is no easy passport to happiness, no automatic assurance of a good and happy and creative life. What it *does* do is to increase the odds enormously.

Some of the people who drink cannot abide the non-drinker. They tell you that you are "socially unacceptable" if you do not drink. They seize every opportunity to convert you to their habits. I spoke not long ago with a beautiful young woman who is a member of Alcoholics Anonymous, an actress by profession. Just one sip of whiskey for her at this point might very well mean the resumption of the chain-reaction of drink and drunkenness. Once it brought her to the point of suicide. It almost ended her career even before that awful night when she turned on the gas-jets in her home.

But do you think that each of her drinking acquaintances accepts and understands her need for total abstention? No—some of them urge her to "try it once again, it won't affect you now." And one was so despicable recently as to put real whiskey in her glass when she was rehearsing a bar-scene for a Broadway show. Had she gulped it down in the belief that it was merely the innocuous, colored liquid normally used on stage, that one gulp might have cost her her life. Fortunately, she smelled the liquor before it was too late, and was saved.

When his friends were with him, Eugene O'Neill drank Coca-Cola from whiskey glasses; thus he was spared their urging to "have just one, it'll make you feel better." At cocktail parties, I carry a glass of ginger ale to avoid being conspicuous. At a dinner party, when I see a glass at my plate, I wait until people are talking and paying no special attention—then I quietly turn my glass upside down. If questioned by a servant, I merely say "No, thank you." If questioned by the hostess, I reply that "It doesn't agree with me." If urged, I add that "I don't care for the taste." If mercilessly prodded and badgered, and my patience gives out, I quietly remark, "You see—my father died of alcoholism."

I cast my vote against social drinking. I will not keep a dog in my house that bites one of every five or nine people who stoop to pet it. Nor will I sanction alcohol because it dooms or harms "just" one of every five, nine or sixteen who drink it.

Look at the list of some of the people whose stories we've seen in this book. These were men and women the world needed—needed until they were seventy, eighty, ninety years of age. Jack London, George Sterling, O. Henry, Stephen Crane, Finley Peter Dunne, Eugene Debs, Sinclair Lewis, Isadora Duncan, William Seabrook, Edna St. Vincent Millay, George Cram Cook, Dylan Thomas, Sherwood Anderson— great people, these, with God-given power to use their minds and bodies for the betterment of our world. When they should have been enjoying their fame, and feeling warm pride at their contributions, they suffered instead.

Too many of them could echo these words by George Sterling:

> *Clear-visioned with betraying night,*
> *I count his merits o'er*
> *And get no comfort from the sight,*
> *Nor any cure therefor.*
> *I'd mourn my desecrated years*
> *(His mained and sorry twin,)*
> *But well he knows my makeshift tears—*
> *The man I might have been.*

17

ONE OF THE most fascinating things in this world is watching how new ideas are born in a free society—how they take root—how like living plants they spread in fertile soil.

An unknown young man named Edison sits in a shop and labors at making threads out of hundreds of different materials; and a few years later, all over the earth, night is turned into day by electricity. Two brothers in a shed behind a bicycle shop figure out the proper shape for an airplane wing, and fifty years later the skies all over the world are filled with jets. These were world-shaking ideas, but the process is just as beautiful, just as vital when the "idea" is the building of a church, a school, a hospital, a public playground. Somebody perceives the need, he gets busy and spreads the idea, a group is wrought and brought together, and the job is put through.

Often there are factions working against each other. Such is the nature of life, such the conflict of motives and ideas. For long years there have been groups fighting against the sale of liquor, and there have been others spending millions to make more millions out of its sale. Yet whether it was legal or illegal, the drinker drank. Victims fell by the wayside, and there was nobody who could help them, no refuge, no care, no hope. That condition existed all through the early years of my life, when the men of my family were being mowed down like grain before the scythe of the harvester. It existed all through my mature years, when my literary friends and colleagues were sharing the same ghastly fate. It existed up to the late thirties.

Then somebody had an idea, and tried it out, and brought a group together, and Alcoholics Anonymous was born.

More than twenty-five years ago, my wife and I made a new friend. He was a vigorous young man, spirited and alert; and when the geography of our careers put many miles between us, we kept in close and continual correspondence through the mails. Then, suddenly, his replies stopped coming. As completely as any person could, he disappeared. It was years before we even heard of him again, and then the news was that he was an alcoholic.

More years passed, and at last a letter came from our friend. And it told us that he no longer drank. These were no idle words, either. Our friend was happy and well and useful. He was cured—he was free.

I wrote to him when this book began to take shape in my mind. He is a writer, a capable craftsman in the communication of ideas and experiences. I told him that I wanted to give my book a "happy ending"—I wanted to end it with his story.

Here is his reply:

> I am flattered that you wish to include me in such illustrious company . . . you seem to have known some of the most gifted drunks of the day. I am free to tell anyone face to face that I am a member of Alcoholics Anonymous. But on the level of the press, the radio and the public platform I must maintain anonymity. Experience has taught us that this is important. There have been some unhappy results when prominent people have broken this rule, and so I must decline. I am so grateful to AA for the new life it has given me, that I could not violate this tradition. All that I am today and all that I can possibly mean to others in the future depends upon my sticking to the AA program in every detail. I was doomed until I found AA. Now I have the health and time to do my work.

Enclosed with my friend's letter were four AA pamphlets. I read them, and then I got the book *Alcoholics Anonymous*. It is a book which opens the gates of hope for the victims of alcoholism—those who want to quit, and those who *want* to want to.

Alcoholics Anonymous, or "AA," as it is known all over the world, celebrated its twentieth anniversary in 1955, with a St. Louis convention attended by 15,000 happy and sober delegates. In all there are more than 6,000 groups with over 200,000 members. Besides, there are nearly 1,000 "Al-Anon Family Groups," where wives and families of alcoholics find help with their problems.

AA was a living idea, and there was need for it, and it spread. The edition of the book which I have was printed in 1950, and it lists thirteen reprintings up to that time; there are more now, and it sells about 25,000 copies yearly. The organization itself increases by about *thirty percent* each year.

Anybody can start a group. There are no dues. The only initiation fee has been paid in long years of subservience to alcohol. Anybody can be a member: AA's are just people who have quit drinking, and who find that they can stay quit by helping others to quit. It is a kind of community enthusiasm which keeps spreading.

They don't get up and shout "Glory, hallelujah!"—they are quiet people, and matter-of-fact about what they are doing, but they feel a glow of satisfaction when they see the thing that worked for them working for others. They are a band of brethren, because they have all been in the same hell and know exactly what it was like down there. They speak and understand a private language, and are pledged, one and all, to come to the rescue of any member who may find himself slipping or threatened with a slip. The weakening member calls one of his brethren, and that person is pledged to drop everything else and come. And when he does come, he knows what to say, because he has been there himself; and the new member knows that he knows, and listens.

AA history dates from Armistice Day, 1934, when Bill W., a World War I veteran and Wall Street broker, launched what was to be the last of the series of brain-shattering benders which for ten years had been dragging him toward destruction. His wife, Lois, sustained until now by her husband's brief periods of sobriety, was on the point of abandoning hope. Their doctor had informed her that the dreaded "wet brain" stage, which would probably mean death or life commitment to an institution, could not be far off.

Lois was keeping things together by working in a department store; hence she was not at home the day an old drinking-crony of Bill's came to call with an exceptional bit of news—he had joined Frank Buchman's Oxford Group, and was sober! Deeply impressed though still tipsy, Bill signed in at a private "drying-out" hospital he'd visited many times before. Here he thought over his friend's suggestions; and although he'd left religion with childhood, Bill W. prayed. There followed an inward experience so startling that he questioned the staff psychiatrist, the late Dr. W. D. Silkworth, about his sanity. The doctor reassured him. Bill emerged from the hospital not only sober, but on fire with a desire to help other alcoholics find sobriety.

For a time his efforts met with consistent failure. Then, while on a business trip to Akron in 1935, he found himself weakening, tempted to drink again. Convinced that he could maintain his own sobriety only by working with drunks, he phoned the Akron churches seeking "prospects." He was put in touch with an alcoholic surgeon, Dr. Bob S.

They were friends on sight. Dr. Bob sobered up, and the two began interminable discussions of the problems of getting sober and remaining so. They agreed that the methods of the Oxford Group did not suit their new purpose, but that certain of the principles it stressed—candor, restitution, humility, and service—were essentials. These were formulated in their famous "Twelve Suggested Steps." Neither Dr. Bob nor Bill W. ever relapsed to drinking. The surgeon died, honored and sober, in 1950. The ex-broker is still active in AA affairs.

From the beginning, their two wives—Dr. Bob's Anne and Bill's Lois—were important partners in the movement. They turned their homes into virtual rescue missions, overflowing with drunks. As more family men entered AA, there were more wives to be encouraged and advised. The book *Alcoholics Anonymous*, from which the society took its name, was published in 1939; and because of Lois's and Anne's experience, special chapters in it were addressed to the needs of wives and families of alcoholics. When the first meetings were held in members' homes, spouses chatted over coffee in the kitchen while the AA's met in the living room. Some wives went along on response to appeals for help ("twelfth step calls"), talking with the sober spouse while the AA members dealt with the inebriate. Later, in localities where the AA tradition includes large "open" (to the public) meetings, non-alcoholic members attended regularly.

It is really the Christian process of conversion, familiar from New Testament days; but it labors to avoid being so labeled. Catholics, Protestants, Jews, Christian Scientists— all are welcome. But so are those persons who dislike "religion" and shy from the word "God" because it means things which seem to them to have no relation to reality. There is a chapter in the book called "We Agnostics," which carefully explains that you can use any name you please for the Higher Power—you may even call it "IT."

Bernard Shaw called it the Life Force, with capital letters, and the French philosopher Bergson called it the *élan vital*, the vital impulse, without capitals. The anonymous authors of *Alcoholics Anonymous* state their conception in this way: "We needed to ask ourselves but one short question: 'Do I now believe, or am I even willing to believe, that there is a Power greater than myself?'" And on that basis they proceeded to lay out a Program of Recovery, of which the first six steps read:

1. We admitted that we were powerless over alcohol—that our lives had become unmanageable.

2. Came to believe that a power greater than ourselves could restore us to sanity.

3. Made a decision to turn our will and our lives over to the care of God as we understood Him.

4. Made a searching and fearless moral inventory of ourselves.

5. Admitted to God, to ourselves and to another human being the exact nature of our wrongs.

6. Were entirely ready to have God remove all these defects of character.

There is a miracle in these six steps. There is a miracle in the decision to "turn our will and our lives over to the care of God."

I have a friend named James H. Richardson; he is city editor of the Los Angeles *Examiner*, and during his astonishing career he has had the task of digging out and telling some of the most sensational crime stories of the past thirty years. There were two interruptions in this career, both of them caused by the fact that Jim was an alcoholic. He tells the story in a book titled *For the Life of Me*, sparing none of the agonies of his experiences.

In it he tells how it all came to an end. Jim was lying in a hospital, in a state of tortured degradation and despair. He heard someone at his bedside, and he looked up. It was the Mother Superior of the hospital, gazing down at him, "her white, white hands interlaced below her silver crucifix." Her words were gentle:

"Is there anything I can do to help?" she asked.

"You can help a lot," Richardson answered. "You can talk to God about me, if you have time."

"That's the only time I have," she said.

Before he left that hospital, Jim Richardson made up his mind that he would never take another drink while he lived. The doctors laughed at him; they had heard this sort of thing before. But faith worked for Richardson, and it has

worked for thousands of members of Alcoholics Anonymous.
Three out of four of the men and women who join the group
recover. Three out of four!

Read the last six steps of the Program for Recovery:

7. (We) humbly asked Him to remove our short-
comings.

8. Made a list of all persons we had harmed and became willing to make amends to them all.

9. Made direct amends to such people whenever possible, except when to do so would injure them or others.

10. Continued to take personal inventory and when
we were wrong, promptly admitted it.

11. Sought through prayer and meditation to improve
our conscious contact with God as we understood Him,
praying only for knowledge of His will for us and the
power to carry that out.

12. Having had a spiritual awakening as the result
of these steps, we tried to carry this message to alcoholics
and to practice these principles in all our affairs.

There it is, you see, the New Life, starting over and over
again in the human soul, the same throughout the ages. It will
go on as long as human life exists; it had to go on if human
life were to begin. It is always choosing new forms, and
especially new names, since the old lose their power by association with human weakness and corruption. Here, among
Americans, it is associated with one practical purpose—the
delivering of human beings from enslavement.

These people of Alcoholics Anonymous have learned
from actual experience what I learned from watching my
alcoholic relatives and friends—that the drink which the
person afflicted with the disease alcoholism cannot take is not
the third nor the fifth nor the eleventh, but the *first*. To
refuse the first, however, he must have help; not merely the
help of friends and associates, but of that mysterious thing

which is hidden in the depths of his own soul, and which doesn't in the least care what name you choose to give It. But it's the same power many of us call our Heavenly Father.

The AA's know how to implement their decision of faith with practical tools and tested advice. The newcomer in their midst sees and hears men and women who were once "dead drunk." He sees their happiness, sees that they are recovered, and he feels their surging drive and compassion. He says, "I can do it too!" If he can be sobered up and kept from drink for just twenty-four hours, he is on the way. He doesn't give up liquor "forever" at this point—just a day at a time, until days becomes weeks and weeks become years. And always there are his brethren, and the practical advice in their book. He can turn to such chapters as "Working with Others," "The Family Afterward," "To Employers," and "A Vision for You." And in it he can read personal stories, much the same in their beginnings as those stories which have appeared in this book of mine. But there's one big difference—the people you read about in the AA book are alive!

For those who are alcoholics—the AA is perhaps the finest answer.

For those who have not yet had their first drink—the wisdom and courage to say "No" is the answer.

For those who have seen the misery and understood the devastation caused by drink — a continuing fight is the answer.

We must fight for a nation in which men and women no longer seek the false stimulation and the fake security, the humbug happiness and the counterfeit strength of liquor. To these ends we must devote our knowledge and our talents and our time.

So long as men are lost to the cup of fury, our fight must continue.

THE CUP OF FURY